SEFER HACHINUCH

ספר החינוך

Selected portions of
Sefer Hachinuch

Annotated and
Translated
by
Rabbi Avraham Yaakov Finkel

YESHIVATH BETH MOSHE
SCRANTON, PA.

CONTENTS

הקדמה
מראש הישיבה
מורינו הרב יעקב שניידמאן שליט"א

מעיקרי ספר החינוך הוא לתת טעם לכל מצוה, ונראה לבאר
שלשה הקדמות הנצרכות להבין ענין של טעמי המצוות.

הראשון, בדרך כלל לכל מצוה יש טעם ועיין רמב"ם הלכות
תמורה פ' ד' וז"ל אע"פ שכל חוקי התורה גזירות הם כמו שביארנו
בסוף מעילה, ראוי להתבונן בהן וכל מה שאתה יכול ליתן לו טעם
תן לו טעם, הרי אמרו חכמים הראשונים שהמלך שלמה הבין רוב
הטעמים של כל חוקי התורה . . . וכל אלו הדברים כדי לכוף את
יצרו ולתקן דעותיו, ורוב דיני התורה אינן אלא עצות מרחוק מגדול
העצה לתקן הדעות ולישר כל המעשים, וכן הוא אומר הלא כתבתי
לך שלישים במועצות ודעת, להודיעך קושט אמרי אמת להשיב
אמרים אמת לשולחך עכ"ל ולפי"ז נבין דלכל מצוה יש טעם לתקן
דעותינו ומעשינו שלא נלכד ברשת החומריות שמטעה האדם. ועוד
יש בהרבה מ"ע ענין להעלות נפשותינו למדריגה עליונה, שמלבד
תיקון המדות פועל המצוה על נפשותינו להתקשר עם עולמות הרוחנ-
יים. והנה קיום המצוה בשלימותה הוא אם מכוין להטעם בשעת
קיומה, או שקודם קיומה מכוין לטעמה ובשעת קיומה ממש יכוין רק
לקיים המצוה. אמנם אף אם לא מכוין להטעם יוצא חיובו. דמ"מ יש
בכח המצוה לפעול בנפשותינו, אבל אין זה קיומה בשלמות.

ענין שני, טעמי המצוות הנזכרים בחינוך לא הוי ביאור לכל פרטי
ההלכות שיש בכל מצוה, אף דהטעם מבאר יסוד בהמצוה מ"מ הרבה
פעמים נמצאים הלכות במצוה שאינם מתישבים לפי הטעם. דבאמת
יש הרבה טעמים בכל מצוה. ועפ"י זה פשוט שאין לפסוק דין עפ"י
הטעמים הנמצאים רק עפ"י דרכי הפסק דנמסר לנו. והא דאיתא דר'
שמעון בן יוחאי היה דורש טעמי דקרא היינו רק אם הטעם מפורש
בתורה ולדעתו הטעם מיותר לדרש. ואף בזה חולקים חכמים עליו.

ענין שלישי, יש כוונה כוללת בכל המצוות והיינו לכוין שהוא
עבד ה' ועושה כל מה שה' מצוה. ובהרבה מצוות נאמר זכר ליציאת
מצרים היינו לזכור שאנו עבדי ה' ואנו עושים כל מה שנצטוינו ואפי'
אם לא היה טעם מבורר לנו. וז"ל הרמב"ן שמות פ' יג' וז"ל ולפיכך
אמרו הוי זהיר במצוה קלה כבחמורה שכולן חמודות וחביבות מאד,
שבכל שעה אדם מודה בהן לאלהיו, וכוונת כל המצות שנאמין
באלהינו ונודה אליו שהוא בראנו, והיא כוונת היצירה, שאין לנו טעם
אחר ביצירה הראשונה, ואין לאל עליון חפץ בתחתונים מלבד שידע
האדם ויודה לאלהיו שבראו, עכ"ל הרי מבואר דיש כונה עיקרי בכל
המצוות והיינו לעשות המצוה מפני שהי"ת ציונו לעשותו, ועי"ז יש
קבלת מלכותו, וקיום אמונה בה'.

הרמב"ם פסק בהל' תפלה וז"ל מי שאמר בתחנונים מי שריחם
על קן ציפור שלא ליקח האם על הבנים או שלא לשחוט אותו ואת
בנו ביום אחד ירחם עלינו וכיוצא בענין זה משתקין אותו, מפני
שמצות אלו גזרת הכתוב הן ואינן רחמים, שאילו היו מפני רחמים
לא היה מתיר לנו שחיטה כל עיקר עכ"ל וקשה דבמורה נבוכים ביאר
דטעם המצוה הוא מפני רחמים. ועוד קשה דהא אף בחוקים יש טעם
כמו שמבואר ברמב"ם שהבאנו. ואמאי לא נאמר שיש טעם של
רחמים בשילוח הקן. ומה שהוכיח משחיטה דלא הוי רחמים צ"ע דהרי
אף בשחיטה יש דינים שנשחוט כדי למעט צער הבהמה. ונראה ליישב
דודאי טעם של רחמים נכלל במצות שילוח הקן, אבל א"א לומר שזהו
יסוד המצוה דודאי יש עוד טעמים נסתרים בהמצוה, ועכ"כ אם אמר
בתפילתו שהקב"ה ירחם עלינו כמו שריחם על קן ציפור הרי ממעט
רחמי שמים עלינו דענין של רחמים במצוה זו הוא רק חלק קטן מן
המצוה, ואדרבא הוא מצמצם במדת הרחמים שהרי בשילוח הקן יש
הרבה דינים שאינם מתאימים עם מדת הרחמים. והרמב"ם בהלכות
מבאר שאנו יודעים דעיקרו הוא חוק ולא משום רחמים דא"כ לא היה
מתיר שחיטה בכלל. ונראה שזה ראיה שאף שיש צדדי רחמים בהמ-
צוה מ"מ יש הרבה צדדים שאינם הולכים עפ"י מדת רחמים.

היוצא מדברינו דכוונה הכוללת בכל מצוה הוא שעושה מפני
ציווי הי"ת בתורת עבדות, ושלמות המצוה הוא שיבין הטעמים
הנכללים בהמצוה. הרחמן הוא יסייע אותנו לעשות כל מצוה
בשלמות האמיתי.

SUMMARY OF
RABBI YAAKOV SCHNAIDMAN'S PROLOGUE

One of the fundamental aims of the Sefer HaChinuch is to provide reasons for the mitzvos. I would like to introduce the following three thoughts as a preface.

Firstly, the Rambam writes, "Although all the laws of the Torah are decrees, it is fitting to delve into them, offering reasons according to one's capabilities. The earlier sages said King Shelomo understood the reason for most of the decrees of the Torah. . . . All the mitzvos constrain the evil inclination and rectify one's character. Indeed, most of the laws of the Torah can be seen as advice from the Great Advisor, to rectify one's character and to make virtuous all one's actions."

The reason for the many prohibitions and commandments is to diminish our inclination and rectify our character, lest we become trapped in physicality, which leads one astray. The positive mitzvos have an additional benefit; they connect us to the spiritual realms. The optimum way to fulfill a mitzvah is to bear in mind the reason while doing it, or to know the reason beforehand, and do the mitzvah with the intention of fulfilling the word of Hashem. However, even one who doesn't know the reason, fulfills his obligation when he does a mitzvah, since mitzvos have inherent power to affect our souls.

Secondly, the reasons mentioned in Sefer HaChinuch define the fundamental ideas of the mitzvah but do not explain its details, and

Rabbi Yaakov Schnaidman is the Rosh Yeshivah of Yeshivath Beth Moshe Scranton, Pennsylvania.

in fact, many details do not conform to the reason given, because there are many correct reasons for the mitzvah. Therefore, we can only formulate a halachah based on the accepted tradition, rather than basing it on a reason, since there are many reasons for each mitzvah. The sages disagreed with Rabbi Shimon who formulated halachos based on the reasons for mitzvos, and even Rabbi Shimon did so only when the reason was found in the Torah indicating that the halachah should follow this reasoning.

Additionally, although the optimum way to fulfill a mitzvah is to understand its reason, nevertheless, there is an intent that pertains to all the mitzvos. One should keep in mind that he is a servant to Hashem, who does His bidding. Many mitzvos are a remembrance for the exodus from Egypt, to remind us that we are His servants doing his bidding. The Mishnah in Avos says, "Be careful with an easy mitzvah as with an important one." The Ramban explains that all mitzvos are very cherished and dear because through each mitzvah one acknowledges Hashem, which is the purpose of every mitzvah and of Creation. The only purpose of Creation is that Man should acknowledge and praise Him.

The Rambam writes that we silence one who says in his supplications, "The one who had mercy on the bird, telling us not to take the mother bird from her young, shall have mercy on us." Or, "The one who had mercy on the animals, telling us not to slaughter a mother and her young on one day, shall have mercy on us." This is because these mitzvos are decrees not merciful prohibitions. Indeed, were they merciful prohibitions, we would not be allowed to slaughter at all. This reasoning is problematic, for the Rambam himself writes in Moreh Nevuchim, that the reason for these mitzvos is because of compassion.

We must realize that although there is a component of mercy in the mitzvah, we cannot say that the basis for all the laws of this mitzvah is mercy, for in fact there are aspects such as slaughtering that are not in line with compassion. If one prays that Hashem should have mercy on us just as He has mercy on the bird, he is limiting the compassion, because compassion is not the only aspect of the mitzvah.

May the Merciful one, help us fulfill every mitzvah in the optimal way.

TRANSLATOR'S INTRODUCTION

Sefer Hachinuch, popularly known as "the *Chinuch*," is a timeless classic that explains the 613 mitzvos in the order in which they appear in the weekly Torah portion. Thus the first mitzvah discussed is, "Be fertile and multiply" (*Bereishis* 1:28); the 613th and last, the mitzvah mandating each Jew to write a *sefer Torah* (*Devarim* 31:19).

The analysis of each mitzvah begins with the quote of its source in the Torah, followed by an exposition of the *shoresh*, the "root" and underlying reason of the mitzvah. This is followed by a review of the relevant aspects of each *halachah*, closing with a summary, outlining where, when, and to whom the mitzvah applies.

The explanations of the *shoresh* of each mitzvah have had a deep impact on Jewish thought making *Sefer Hachinuch* a popular work ever since it was first printed (Venice, 1523).

A noteworthy feature of the *Chinuch* is the author's introduction in which he proves the truth of the Torah and reviews various elements of *hashkafah*—the Torah outlook on life. Explaining his reason for writing the *sefer*, the author says, ". . . it is meant to inspire my young son and his friends to find the number of mitzvos in the Torah portion they learn every week, rather than playing silly and pointless games. Instead, they will ask each other, 'How many mitzvos are there in this week's *parasha*?'"

Thus, many of the *Chinuch*'s comments begin with the phrase, "My dear son, you should know . . ." This fatherly approach sets the gentle tone for the entire work.

THE AUTHOR OF SEFER HACHINUCH

Out of his great modesty, the author of *Sefer Hachinuch* did not disclose his name. Some scholars attribute the work to Rabbi Aharon HaLevi of Barcelona (1235-1290), [known as *Ra'ah*,] a prominent *rishon* (early Talmudic authority) who wrote many important *sefarim*. These [scholars] base their assumption on a phrase in the *Chinuch*'s introduction where the author describes himself as, "a Jewish man of the house of Levi, from Barcelona." Others disagree, noting that a number of halachic rulings in the *Chinuch* are at odds with opinions the *Ra'ah* expresses in his writings; thus the *Ra'ah* could not be the author of the *Chinuch*. The question of authorship is still unresolved.

Rabbi Yosef Babad of Tarnopol (1800-1874) wrote an extensive commentary on *Sefer Hachinuch*, entitled *Minchas Chinuch* (Lemberg, 1869). It is an indispensable aid to understanding the halachic topics in the *Chinuch*.

The present volume contains a selection of mitzvos discussed in the *Chinuch*, citing their source in the Torah and their *shoresh*—the "root" or reason for the mitzvah. However, the intricate halachic particulars relating to the mitzvah are omitted.

May this translation provide you with a deeper understanding of the mitzvos and a strong commitment to *limud haTorah*, and may it give you a taste of the greatness of *Sefer Hachinuch* and encourage you to study the full text.

AVRAHAM YAAKOV FINKEL
Kislev 5771/'10

SEFER HACHINUCH

ספר החינוך

A Letter by the Author

=⊷◉⊶=

Studying this *sefer,* the reader may be led to believe that the author with toil and intellectual prowess gathered all its laws from the words of the Talmudic Sages. If this were true, the author would have to be thoroughly familiar with the full range of Talmudic literature. [The author,] knowing himself and recognizing his limited wisdom, [wishes] to set the record straight and make the truth known to one and all. Thereby he will not do G-d's work under false pretenses, and will not—with malice and deception—take credit for the achievements of others, acting like a weakling wearing the armor of a champion, like a good-for-nothing adorning himself with a royal crown.

And so, the author herewith publicly declares and testifies to everyone who reads this work that most of the contents of this *sefer* are taken from the works of Rabbi Yitzchak Alfasi (Rif) and Rabbi Moshe b. Maimon (Rambam), both universally acclaimed illustrious Sages. They deserve the major part of the glory and honor for this work. Recognition is due also to the celebrated and erudite Rabbi Moshe b. Nachman (Ramban) who wrote a highly regarded *sefer* on the count of the mitzvos, in addition to many other fine works.

They are the early Talmudic authorities who devoted most of their time to clarifying the words of the Talmudic Sages, probing the depths of the mighty waters [of the Talmud], extracting pearls from the words of the Gemara. And when we entered their sanctuary and the chamber of their teachings, we found there a wellspring of fresh water, gardens and orchards, pastries and silk garments ready for the taking.

How can I expect these outstanding Sages to approve of my work when they themselves have already explained all these matters? [I concluded that they will favor my work] because I arranged the 613 mitzvos in the order of the weekly portion in which they appear. Perhaps as a result, the youngsters will find them fascinating and pay attention to them on Shabbos and Yom Tov, thereby being educated in the light of Torah life rather than behaving boisterously in the streets. The young boys will ask each other: "How many mitzvos are there in this week's *parashah*?" As a result, the earth will be filled with knowledge and prudence.

Here, the explanation of every mitzvah is laid out before them, and without effort they will find delightful explanations in the chapters of this *sefer*.

May G-d bless His holy people with their children and all that is theirs wherever they may reside, and may I be included with them in this blessing.

By the Name of Hashem I bind by oath every copyist [of this *sefer*] to write this letter at the beginning, and may he be blessed for this with life and peace. For [the purpose of this letter is] that all [readers] may attribute glory and splendor to [the Rif, Rambam, and Ramban] its originators. Whoever corrects an error in it after studying it thoroughly, may he receive his full reward from G-d, and peace upon Yisrael.

AUTHOR'S OVERVIEW

THE REVELATION AT SINAI

If something is accepted by most people, it is usually considered absolute truth. People have unanimously accepted the testimony of witnesses, and the more witnesses that testify to a matter, the more convinced people are of its truth. When only a few witnesses attest to a matter, intelligent people have doubts about it. This principle is so firmly established, that every nation mandates capital punishment through the testimony of two or—even better— three witnesses. The Torah of Moshe decrees likewise.

For this reason, mankind accepted the testimony of fathers and grandfathers about events that happened earlier. Children will certainly accept and believe something when their fathers testify that something occurred which they and many others saw with their own eyes. Therefore, G-d gave the Torah to His people Yisrael in the presence of 600,000 grown men, not to mention the great number of women and children. Thus, we have many faithful witnesses to the event.

To strengthen the testimony, making it even more trustworthy, all Yisrael was also granted prophecy, since things revealed through prophecy can never be doubted. Therefore, Hashem said to Moshe, *"I will come to you in a thick cloud, so that the people will hear when I speak to you, and they will then believe in you forever"*(*Shemos* 19:9). He implied that they and their children will

5

believe in Moshe and his prophecy forever, knowing with absolute certainty that G-d can speak with man and he will survive, and moreover, that all Moshe's prophecy is true.

Despite all the wondrous signs Moshe performed before Pharaoh and Bnei Yisrael, had they not attained the level of prophecy, doubters might have argued, "Perhaps Moshe did everything by conjuring up demons, or through the power of the names of angels?"

Even though the wise men and sorcerers of Egypt, who were more knowledgeable in demonology and sorcery than the rest of the world, admitted to Pharaoh that Moshe worked with the power of Hashem, as it says, *The sorcerers said to Pharaoh, "This is the finger of G-d"* (*Shemos* 8:15), an obstinate scoffer can still say [it was only because Moshe's] knowledge of sorcery was superior to [Pharaoh's sorcerers] that they conceded to him. But Yisrael had no doubts at all since they attained the level of prophecy and knew with complete certainty that all [Moshe's] deeds were done by order of the Master of the universe, and through His power everything happened to them.

Witnessing the revelation at Sinai with their own eyes, and thereby knowing with total certainty that it is truthful, [the Jews] bore witness to the children born afterwards that all the words of the Torah which they received through Moshe, from the first letter of *Bereishis* to the last letter of *le'einei kol Yisrael,* are true and certain beyond a shadow of a doubt. Their children, in turn, bore witness to their children, and their children to their children, and so on, until today.

The Torah in our hands is a Torah of truth based on the word of 600,000 faithful witnesses, which includes people with every conceivable human characteristic—not counting women and children.

Should a non-believer try to mislead you, saying, "Dear Jew, what good is your tradition? Why base your belief on you father's and grandfather's words? Do your own research, thinking for yourself. Look at the movement of the zodiac and the four elements that exist on earth, and you will understand the secrets of wisdom, discovering how the One and only created this unique [universe]."

We answer, that we will never grasp anything about the essence of G-d from our own probing. Even in this lowly world scientists cannot fully understand everything. Who has discovered through physical science the properties of herbs and fruits, the [chemical] composition of gems and precious stones, or why a magnet attracts iron? These [questions] have baffled all scientists and philosophers.

Even if we understand some science and philosophy, we should not, G-d forbid, arrogantly reflect on the essence of G-d, and contemplate things that are beyond human comprehension and which are not necessary. Our forefathers gave us the answer on a silver platter. Through deep reflection they attained the ultimate truth, concluding that G-d speaks to man and he can survive. Since they [told us] the truth, why should we analyze their words? [All we need to do is] thirstily drink their words as they are recorded in the written text.

A parable: A man was warned by thousands of people not to drink water from a certain river, since its waters kill those who drink from it. The water had been tested a thousand times, at different occasions, and by people from different countries. One learned doctor told him, "Don't believe them. In my professional opinion this water is not toxic rather it is pure and rapid-flowing, with good soil in the riverbed. Drink it to your heart's content." Would it be advisable for him to ignore the unanimous testimony of everyone else, to follow the doctor's recommendation? Of course not; a sensible person would not listen to [the doctor] nor follow his suggestion.

The truth about the nature of the world is established by the testimony of a far greater number of people, than the scientists who theorize with reasoning and abstract thinking. Since man is not perfect, his mind cannot fathom the essence of things. It is best that man act according to the words of the Torah that the Master of wisdom gave to man, and which we received from trustworthy witnesses. It contains all precious knowledge and all magnificent wisdom.

GIVING THE TORAH TO HUMANS

Perhaps one will ask, "Why did Hashem give the precious Torah to human beings? Everything belongs to Hashem, and His grandeur and glory are unexcelled. Informing people of the power of His deeds does not add to His honor, for nothing can be added to or subtracted from supreme glory and splendor."

The answer is simple: The human mind cannot grasp the ways of its Creator nor know why He performs His deeds, for His ways are higher than their ways and His thoughts are higher than their thoughts. We do not know the reason [Hashem entrusted us with the Torah,] yet we believe that the Father of wisdom, the Master of all, did everything for a purpose and an important aim.

Nevertheless we can attempt to give a partial reason for this. Hashem's lofty distinction necessitated that man can have knowledge of the ways of Hashem. Since He decided to create the world, it follows that [the world] is perfect, for the deeds of one who is perfect are perfect. And in truth He created a perfect world, which is complete without lacking anything. No one can say about His world, "Why didn't He make it easier for more of His wisdom to be known from His world?"

In His world He created intangible thinking beings, namely angels, and He also created thinking entities - the heaven and its array. On earth, He created bodily creatures without thinking power; animals, birds, and similar species. He also created earthly, physical beings with intelligence, the human race, which manifests that nothing is impossible for Him. Even though matter and intelligence are polar opposites, with His great wisdom, He merged them into one, making man. This [creature] which combines intelligence and matter should certainly know his Creator and acknowledge Him, thereby bringing to fruition [G-d's] intention in creating him.

If not for the Torah that G-d gave him, man's intelligence would gravitate toward his physical nature and its desires; he would be likened to the dumb animals. Then the work [of Creation] would not be complete, for the human body and the animal would be similar, even though they are not identical in form, and Creation would be flawed. Thus, the Torah which imparts wisdom to man, was indispensable for the completion of Creation.

Perhaps you may ask, "Since [the Torah] is the fulfillment of Creation, why was it only given to one people among the nations of the world, rather than everyone?" Again, the answer is simple: Though the mind of man who is the product of creation cannot comprehend the mind of the Creator, we can understand this with an analogy to the nature of the world.

In this lowly world there is always more waste matter than core matter during production, and only a fragment finally becomes the finished product. Similarly most fields in the world are not arable; and of the arable lands, only a small fraction of them have prime soil. The same is true for the produce of the world and the species of domestic animals and fowl.

This principle must also apply to mankind, since man with his mortal body is comparable to other species in this lowly world. Therefore, one segment of the human race, Yisrael, the smallest of all nations was chosen. Blessed be Hashem for recognizing them as the elite and for calling them His people, giving them the fundamental principles of wisdom. And among the people of Yisrael, one group is distinguished—the tribe of Levi who was chosen to serve Him continually,.

However, He also gave an opportunity to the rest of humanity to elevate themselves from the animals through the seven mitzvos commanded to all people of the world, which we will write about with G-d's help.

The same holds true on our planet earth, one portion is more select than the rest. Because Eretz Yisrael is outstanding, Hashem desired that the elite of humanity settle there. In Eretz Yisrael, the best place is Yerushalayim therefore it was selected to be the dwelling-place of the Torah and the site chosen for the worship of G-d. From there, the entire earth is blessed, *for there Hashem commanded the blessing* (*Tehillim* 133:3).

The Jews in Exile

Why do the Jewish people, the chosen portion, suffer exile and misery since ancient times? All the people of the world know, that the Master of all, created two worlds; a physical and a spiritual universe. They also know that the physical world is insignificant compared to the spiritual world, for [the physical world] is like a fleeting shadow, whereas [the spiritual world] endures for all eternity. Since the soul is the part of man that lives forever, whereas the body serves the soul for a short time and then disintegrates, Hashem granted His people the spiritual world, an eternal world of boundless delight, as an inheritance.

Why did G-d not give both portions—the joys of the spiritual and the physical worlds—to His chosen nation?

Every intelligent person knows that a man of flesh and blood cannot live forever without sinning. Furthermore, he knows that one of the unchanging attributes of G-d, is Justice. This obligates every intelligent person to follow a wise way of life, and to be guilty to [G-d] the King when he strays. Once the Attribute of Justice finds him guilty, it is impossible for Him to wipe the slate clean. Therefore, out of Hashem's gracious kindness, He enabled us to atone for our sins in this fleeting world, so our souls may be pure and everlasting in the world of the souls. For one hour there is more magnificent than all life in this world.

However, in time to come, the time of Mashiach, we will be worthy of both worlds. At that time we will not need to have our bodies purified, for our evil impulse will be nullified, as it says, *I will remove the heart of stone from your flesh* (*Yechezkel* 36:26). Should a trace of sin remain, the guilt will be shifted to the head of the scapegoat [which is sent to its death on Yom Kippur] as in former times [when the Beis Hamikdash was standing].

Indeed, it says in the Torah, *If you follow My laws* (*Vayikra* 26:3) I will bestow on you the goodness of this world. This means, if you are perfect, with no need to purify your body, you will also deserve the goodness of this world. And so it says about Avraham, *Hashem blessed Avraham with everything* (*Bereishis* 24:1), meaning, [He blessed him] also with the goodness of this world, for he did not need to purify his body at all.

With this [explanation] you will realize that it is for their own benefit and honor that the Jews suffer in exile more than any other nation. This is an important concept which wicked men do not understand; only an intelligent person can grasp it. Many impoverished Jews, plagued by the miseries of the exile, cannot understand the goodness of the spiritual world. Collapsing under the weight of their worries, they are unable to think straight. May Hashem in His kindness remove evil thoughts from our hearts, bestowing on us proper insight and a correct outlook on life so His desire for our perfection will be realized. Amein, may He do so.

THE WORLD TO COME

Perhaps you will wonder, why doesn't G-d state in the Torah, "If you keep My mitzvos, I will give you [a share] in the World to Come"?

The concept of the World to Come is obvious to every intelligent person. No nation denies life in the hereafter, nor does anyone deny that the greater the goodness, wisdom, and good deeds of a soul, the greater is its delight [in the World to Come]. For the intelligent soul stems from the [heavenly] source of intelligence, and the closer it approaches its origin, the greater is its delight.

These things do not need support through proofs and witnesses; they are self-evident. The Torah doesn't elaborate on things that can be acquired by the human intellect. Indeed, the Sages said in many places, "This is a reasonable assumption," meaning, there is no need for a supporting verse for something dictated by logic.

Therefore, the Torah [only] promised us reward for keeping the mitzvos in this world. We will not be hampered by earning our livelihood or by war with enemies, so we can serve G-d and fulfill His will. The Torah does not need to elaborate further saying, "And when you do His will, you will merit attaining the delight of the World to Come." It is self-understood that every individual

who fulfills the will of his Creator will be brought closer to Him
and delight in His radiance.

But, had the Torah only promised us a reward in the World to
Come, and not a reward in this world, the promise would not be
evident in this life, and it might raise qualms in the minds of people of wavering faith.

FUNDAMENTAL TENETS OF THE TORAH

One of the fundamental principles of the Torah which Hashem
gave His people through His prophet Moshe, is to know that
Hashem, our G-d in heaven above, Who gave this Torah to Yisrael,
is the First Being; His existence is without beginning or end. He
brought everything that exists into being, creating everything by
His will and power, out of nothing. Whatever He created will exist
as long as He wishes and not a moment longer. No task is beyond
His capability. We must believe that He is One and no other being
is associated with Him; that by fulfilling what is written in the
Torah, one's soul will merit everlasting delight; and that G-d oversees the behavior of all humanity, and knowing in detail all their actions rewards everyone according his deeds.

Another fundamental tenet of the Torah is the belief that the
true interpretation of the Torah is the traditional explanation we
received from the early Jewish authorities. Any comment that con-
tradicts their interpretation is false and worthless, for the Sages received the meaning of the Torah from Moshe, who received it from
Hashem when he stayed on the mountain for forty days. Though
the [Divine] Teacher could have taught Moshe in less time,
Hashem hinted to [future] students that they must spend time
studying the Torah discerningly and judiciously.

The authentic interpretation is found in the Babylonian and
Jerusalem Talmud composed by our early Sages, who received it
generation after generation from Moshe Rabbeinu. Because the
Babylonian Talmud is larger and easier to understand than the
Jerusalem Talmud, we rely more heavily on it. It is divided into six

orders comprising sixty tractates, each dealing each dealing with a particular subject. There is a total of 522 chapters.

The true meaning of the Torah may also be found in other works known as *Sifra, Sifrei, Tosefta,* and *Mechilta,* written by our early rabbinic Sages. These works are accepted by all Yisrael, and their contents are relied on without any dissenting opinion. The Sages explained how to reconcile opposing views. Everything is crystal clear, with no doubt or confusion for those who understand [the issue at hand].

Whoever doubts these interpretations, is not true to the beliefs of the holy nation [of Yisrael,] for we can never draw the correct inference by [reading] the simple meaning of the Torah text. There are many verses in the Torah that seem to contradict each other, but one who knows their explanation, understands and agrees that *the ways of Hashem are straight* (*Hoshea* 14:10).

For example, it says, *The time that B'nei Yisrael dwelled in Egypt lasted 430 years* (*Shemos* 12:40). Yet, if you add the years of Kehos, son of Levi, who went down [from Canaan] to Egypt and the years of his son Amram, and the eighty years of [Amram's son] Moshe— who was eighty years old when he stood before Pharaoh—the total is only 350 years! Our sages explain that the count of 430 years started from the time Avraham was told, *Know for sure that your descendants will be foreigners in a land that is not theirs for 400 years* (*Bereishis* 15:13). We understand the verse as follows, *The time that B'nei Yisrael dwelled in Egypt* and in other lands [from the time their exile began,] *lasted 430 years.* As soon as Avraham was told, *Your descendants will be foreigners . . .* he began to feel the pain [of exile], therefore the count begins at that point in time.

Although the verse says, *B'nei Yisrael,* which means the descendants of Yisrael [and Avraham was not a descendant of Yisrael,] the Midrash says Avraham was called Yisrael. Thus, we understand the verse as if it said "B'nei Yisrael and Yisrael," since the Father [Avraham] felt the pain of his descendants when [G-d] announced the exile of his descendants.

The phrase *dwelled in Egypt,* is not meant literally [because they dwelled in other places besides Egypt]. The Torah says *in Egypt,* because they spent the main part of the exile there, and composites are always named for their main component.

Similarly, it says, *Your ancestors immigrated to Egypt with seventy souls* (*Devarim* 10:22), yet counting them individually, you find only 69 persons. This is explained because Yocheved was born between the [double] walls [that formed the border of Egypt. Thus they left with 69 people but arrived with 70].

Similarly, one verse says, *Eat matzos for seven days* (*Shemos* 12:15), and another verse says, *Six days eat matzah* (*Devarim* 16:8). [*Rashi* explains that matzah of the *new* crop may not be eaten until after the *omer* offering was brought on the second day of Pesach, thus it could only be eaten for six days.] There are many such examples, where the verse cannot be understood without the traditional Torah commentary transmitted to us from Moshe Rabbeinu.

THE 613 MITZVOS

According to our tradition and the commentaries we received from our Sages, the number of mitzvos in the Torah that Hashem gave us and which remain in effect for all generations, totals 613 mitzvos. They comprise 248 [positive] mitzvos that He commanded us to do, and 365 [negative] mitzvos that He cautioned against doing—all are called mitzvos.

All Jews—both men and women—are required to do some of the mitzvos in every place and at every time. Other mitzvos are incumbent only on Yisraelim, but not on kohanim and levi'im. There are mitzvos that only levi'im must observe, while other mitzvos are kept only by kohanim, in every place and at every time. Then there are mitzvos that only a king of Yisrael must observe. Some mitzvos are commanded to the community as a whole to observe, but not an individual. Still other mitzvos must be observed only in a certain place and at a certain time—in Eretz Yisrael, when most of the Jews in the world are there. Even then, the obligation to observe certain mitzvos is different for men and women, for Yisraelim, kohanim and levi'im.

Some of the mitzvos are incumbent on a person all the time, such as the mitzvah to love Hashem and be in awe of Him, and mitzvos similar to this. We are required to do other mitzvos only at a designated time—such as the mitzvah of *sukkah, lulav, shofar,* abstaining from work on the Yamim Tovim, reciting the *Shema,* and so on. These mitzvos must be performed at a set time of the year or the day.

There are some mitzvos a person does not observe unless an occasion arises requiring him to do that mitzvah, such as paying a worker on time. Surely no one is required to hire workers merely to fulfill this mitzvah. There are other such mitzvos which we will discuss in their place with Hashem's help.

The mitzvah of Torah study is the foundation of all mitzvos, since by learning the Torah, a person will know the mitzvos and be able to fulfill them. For this reason the Sages decreed that in the synagogue where people gather, we read one portion of the Torah each week, until the entire *sefer Torah* is completed. Thus, every week the people are inspired with the words of the Torah and mitzvos. Most of today's communities follow the custom of reading the entire Torah each year.

Furthermore, our Sages urged every Jew to read [the portion of the week] that is read in the synagogue, at home as well. This is how they put it, "A person should always complete [his reading] of the Torah portion of the week along with the congregation," so that, having read it at home he will understand it better.

RATIONALE FOR THE MITZVOS

The 613 mitzvos are scattered in different places throughout the Torah, at times they are placed among stories that were written for the important principles and essential [moral] teachings they convey. Because the reader might not realize how many mitzvos he has read that week, and may not be inspired to do them with fervor, I, the most insignificant among the Torah scholars of my time, a Jew of the house of Levi of the city of Barcelona, thought it worthwhile to write the mitzvos in the order in which they appear in the weekly Torah portion, in order to excite my young son and his friends to find the number of mitzvos in the Torah portion they learn every week, training them to focus their mind on pure thoughts and meaningful calculations, rather than silly and trivial games. Then, even when they grow old, they will not swerve from it.

I wish to write one underlying reason for each mitzvah. When [the reason] is expressly revealed in the Torah, I will quote the relevant verse, and when [the reason] is not revealed, I will relate what I have heard from Torah scholars and from my own understanding of the subject matter. I do not presume to arrive at the truth in every case, for I am not a man but a worm, who has never seen the light of wisdom. How dare I grapple with matters that learned sages have not grasped? I understand that ants cannot carry the burden of camels, and that a child who does not know to Whom the berachos are said, cannot give a lecture on the Works of the Heavenly Chariot and the mystery of the angel Chashmal. Only, my insatiable desire to "dip the tip of my staff into the honeycomb" drove me to enter the endless forest, even though I know many great men have entered there only to come up with charcoal.

But I said to myself: If my mind will be occupied with this all my life, I will not become damaged and tainted by corrupt schemes and wrongdoing like [the minds] of the sinful evildoers.

I will set the mitzvos as a signet ring on my right hand, dedicating all my resources to performing them all day, making a faithful home and a sturdy dwelling for them in my heart.

All my other activities—eating, drinking, and dealing with [the problems] of men and women—I will do in due time.

The mitzvos are all purified and clean, "their canopy is of every precious stone," and if you sometimes find inferior matter in the commentary that is written about them, select the "the edible food" and return [the scraps] to the owner's house. Whoever wishes to dine with me, can eat the meat and leave the bones and the shells on the table.

I justify writing my work, because my teachers said, "All small talk is bad, but small talk about Torah is good." Furthermore, about the verse, *His banner of love was over me,* our Sages explain that even a child's stammering is pleasing to Hashem, [for the Hebrew word for *banner* is *diglo,* which is similar to the word *lilugo* which means to stammer.]

MITZVAH 1 ~ מצוה א

TO BE FRUITFUL AND MULTIPLY

—————◆◆◆—————

I t is a mitzvah to marry a woman in order to have children, as it says, *G-d blessed them, saying to them, "Be fertile and multiply"* (*Bereishis* 1:28).

A fundamental reason for this mitzvah is to populate the world since Hashem, blessed be He, wants it to be inhabited, as it says, *He did not create it for emptiness; He fashioned it to be inhabited* (*Yeshayah* 45:18). Through this important mitzvah, all the mitzvos in the world, which were given to human beings not to ministering angels, can be fulfilled.[1]

By failing to marry, one is ignoring a positive commandment, [an offense] for which one incurs very great punishment, since he implicitly shows that he does not want to fulfill Hashem's will to settle His world.

---

[1] If people do not have children, there will be no one to fulfill the mitzvos.

MITZVAH 2 ~ מצוה ב

THE MITZVAH OF CIRCUMCISION

━━━━●◖◗●━━━━

There is a mitzvah of circumcision, as it says, *This is My covenant that you shall guard between Me and between you and your offspring. You must circumcise every male (Bereishis 17:10).*

The foreskin covering the tip of the male organ is cut away, and the thin membrane beneath [the foreskin] is removed, baring the head of the organ. Wise men know that the human form attains perfection by removing the foreskin, for it is a useless appendage.

Hashem, may He be blessed, wished to affix a permanent sign on the bodies of the people He set apart to be called by His Name. Thus they are distinguished from the other nations in their body, just as they are different in their spiritual outlook, conduct, and demeanor. This physical differentiation was set in the male organ of reproduction which ensures the continued existence of mankind. This is in addition to the fact that it brings the human body to perfection, as we mentioned above.

Though Hashem wanted the [physical] form of the Chosen People to be perfect, He wanted the process of perfection to be carried out by man himself. He did not create [man] complete and perfect at birth, to signify that just as man can attain physical perfection through his own hands, so too, he can refine his soul through his virtuous actions.

MITZVAH 3 ~ מצוה ג

NOT TO EAT THE DISPLACED THIGH NERVE

⸻◦⊙◦⸻

We are prohibited to eat the *gid hanasheh* [the thigh nerve], as it says [in the narrative of Yaakov fighting with the angel,] *and therefore B'nei Yisrael do not eat the displaced nerve on the hip joint* (*Bereishis* 32:33).

This mitzvah suggests that even though Yisrael will suffer extreme hardship at the hands of the nations and the descendants of Eisav when they are in exile, they can rest assured that they will not perish. Their offspring and name will endure forever, and a redeemer will deliver them from their oppressor. Keeping this thought constantly in mind through this mitzvah, they will remain steadfast in their faith and righteousness forever.

The angel who wrestled with our father Yaakov was the guardian angel of Eisav attempting to eliminate Yaakov and his offspring from the world. Unable to defeat Yaakov, he disabled him by touching the socket of his thigh. Similarly, the descendants of Eisav inflict pain and suffering on the descendants of Yaakov, but ultimately Yaakov will be rescued from Eisav, thus it says about Yaakov, *the sun rose and was shining on him* to heal him, delivering him from his distress. So too, the sun of Mashiach will shine for us, healing us from our suffering and redeeming us speedily in our days—*Amein.*

MITZVAH 16 ~ מצוה טז

NOT TO BREAK THE BONES OF
THE PESACH OFFERING

———◦◉◦———

We are forbidden to break any bone of the Pesach offering, as it says, *Do not break any of its bones* (*Shemos* 12:46).

This mitzvah reminds us of the miracles of Egypt, as we mentioned in connection with the other [mitzvos of Pesach]. It is not proper for the members of royalty and their cabinet to scrape and crack bones like dogs, the way starving paupers do. Therefore, as soon as we became the special treasure of all nations—a kingdom of priests and a holy nation—and every anniversary thereof, it is appropriate that we do actions that recall the lofty status we attained at that time. Through the symbolic acts we perform, this matter becomes ingrained permanently in our souls.

My son, do not ask: Why did Hashem Yisbarach command us to do many [mitzvos] to commemorate the miracle [of the exodus from Egypt?] Wouldn't one reminder suffice for us and our descendants to remember it forever? It is not with wisdom, rather it is childish, to ask thus.

My son, lend an ear to listen with understanding and I will teach you to benefit from Torah and mitzvos.

Man is influenced by his actions; his heart and thoughts are always swayed by the activities he is engaged in, for good or for bad. Even a person who is wicked to the core, and whose every impulse of his innermost thoughts is evil all day, will immediately change course for the good if he sets his mind to persistently study Torah and do mitzvos, even were it not for the sake of Heaven. The power of his good deeds will subdue his evil impulse, for the heart is drawn by one's actions.

And if a perfectly upright and honest tzaddik, who only desires Torah and mitzvos, becomes constantly occupied in immoral matters, perhaps because the king forcibly appointed him to an unsavory post, he will eventually become totally corrupt because working at this post constantly taints his righteous heart, for as we said above, man is influenced by his actions.

Therefore the Sages of blessed memory said: The Omnipresent wished to confer merit on Yisrael, therefore He gave them an abundance of Torah and mitzvos, so that all our thoughts and actions will be focused on the mitzvos, for our ultimate good. Our good actions cause us to become good, thereby becoming worthy of everlasting life. Our Sages of blessed memory alluded to this when they said, "Whoever has a *mezuzah* at his entrance, *tzitzis* on his garment, and *tefillin* on his head, is assured that he will not sin." These continual mitzvos exert a lasting hold on a person.

Therefore, choose your occupation carefully, for it will influence you. Don't allow your evil impulse to persuade you by saying, "Since my belief in G-d is firm and unshakeable, what harm is there if I occasionally indulge in mundane pleasures, lingering in markets and streets, bantering with scorners, telling witty jokes, and doing other things that are not sinful? Surely, my heart is as strong as theirs, my little finger is thicker than their loins.[2] How can they lure me into following them?"

My son! Beware, lest you be trapped in their snare. Many who thought along these lines have drunk their cup of poison. But you my son, must save your soul.

Now, you will not find it hard to understand why there are so many mitzvos commemorating the miracles of Egypt. They are a major pillar in our Torah, and the more we are occupied with them, the more we are influenced by them.

---

2   1 *Melachim* 12:10.

MITZVAH 18 ~ מצוה יח

To Sanctify the Firstborn in Eretz Yisrael

———⊙———

We are commanded to sanctify the firstborn. Every newborn male that is the first to emerge from the womb, whether human or animal, is holy to Hashem, as it says, *Sanctify to Me every firstborn. The first issue of every womb among B'nei Yisrael, both of man and of beast, is Mine* (*Shemos* 13:2).

Hashem granted us the merit of performing a mitzvah with the "first of our fruit," so we will realize that everything belongs to Him, and everything a man has in this world is allotted to him through Hashem's kindness. He comes to this realization when seeing that he labors very hard, and endures a great deal of discomfort, yet when the time comes to reap the fruit, he immediately gives the first of his fruit, which is as dear to him as the apple of his eye, to the Holy One, blessed be He, divesting himself of his possession, handing it over to His Creator.

[Another reason for this mitzvah is] to remember the great miracle that Hashem performed for us, [killing] the firstborn of Egypt and saving us from their hand.

MITZVAH 21 ~ מצוה כא

TO TELL THE STORY OF THE DEPARTURE FROM EGYPT

[I]t is a mitzvah] to talk about the departure from Egypt, each person according to his command of the language, on the evening of the fifteenth of Nissan, lauding and praising Hashem for all the miracles He performed for us there. As it says, *On that day you must tell your son, "It is because of this, that Hashem acted for me when I left Egypt"* (*Shemos* 13:8).

We have received many mitzvos, commands and prohibitions, about [remembering the exodus] because it is a fundamental and integral principle of our Torah and faith. In all our berachos and prayers we say, "a memorial of the Exodus from Egypt," since [the exodus] is an indisputable sign and proof that the world was created out of nothing, and that there is an able and willing G-d who preceded [every being that was created]. He brought everything into being, and everything depends on His existence. He has the power to change [all creations] at will whenever He wishes as He did in Egypt, changing the laws of nature for our sake and performing great, mighty, and unparalleled signs. This refutes all those who deny the creation of the world out of nothing, confirming belief in Hashem and the doctrine that His providence and power touches one and all.

MITZVAH 25 ~ מצוה כה

To Believe in Hashem

———◦◉◦———

We must believe that the world has one G-d, who brought into being everything that exists; everything that was, that is, and that will be, happens by His power and His will for all eternity; and He brought us out of Egypt, giving us the Torah. *I am Hashem, your G-d, who brought you out of Egypt, from the place of slavery* (*Shemos* 20:2), means, "You shall know and believe that the world has a G-d." The word, *I*, denotes His existence. The words, *brought you out of Egypt*, teach, "Do not think your escape from Egyptian bondage and the plagues that beset the Egyptians happened by chance."

It is self-understood that this belief is the foundation of our religion. Whoever does not believe in it denies the basic principles of our faith, and has no share or merit in Yisrael.

This mitzvah demands that one plant positively in his mind, that this is the truth, and that nothing else is possible. He must commit himself to answer any challenger, that he truly believes this in his heart, and will never accept anything else even if he is threatened with death. By turning something that lies dormant in one's heart into reality, he strengthens and solidifies his deep-seated belief. Thus, by affirming with his words what his heart has decided, [one reinforces one's faith]. If he advances in wisdom, to understand with undeniable proof that the belief he holds is the truth and nothing but the truth, he will then fulfill this mitzvah in the best possible way.

MITZVAH 31 ~ מצוה לא

To Sanctify the Shabbos with Spoken Words

[T]his mitzvah requires us] to speak words about Shabbos at its beginning and at its end, alluding to the day's greatness, loftiness, and praiseworthiness, that set it apart from all other days. For it says, *Remember the Shabbos day to keep it holy* (*Shemos* 20:8), meaning, remember it by recalling its holiness and greatness.

Kiddush inspires us to remember the greatness of the day, implanting in our hearts belief in the creation of the world out of nothing, as it says, *for it was during the six weekdays that Hashem made the heavens, the earth, the sea and all that is in them, but He rested on Shabbos* (*Shemos* 20:11).

We were commanded to perform [*Kiddush* and *Havdalah*] with wine, for [wine] satisfies and gladdens a person, strongly stimulating his senses, and man's character is formed according to the fervor with which he acts.

In light of the above, our Sages said that a person who likes bread more than wine should recite the *Kiddush* on bread, since he will be more inspired with something he likes better. However, they did not [permit using bread] for *Havdalah*, requiring one to make *Havdalah* over wine regardless of his preference. Like our perfect Torah, they always follow the majority; and in truth, most people would rather drink than eat after Shabbos, since they ate a big meal during the day in honor of Shabbos.

25

MITZVAH 32 ~ מצוה לב

NOT TO WORK ON SHABBOS

We are forbidden to work on Shabbos, nor may we allow our children, servants, and animals to work, as it says, *Do not do anything that constitutes work. [This includes] you, your son, your daughter, your servant, your maid, your animal, and the foreigner in your gates* (*Shemos* 20:10).

We neglect our usual occupation in honor of the day, to implant in our minds belief in the creation of the world out of nothing, since this belief incorporates all the fundamental principles of our faith. Week after week on this day we will remember that the world was created in six days, and on the seventh day nothing was created. On each day different things were created, demonstrating [that the world was created] solely by [Divine] will, as opposed to the ideology of the despised thinkers who [falsely] reason that although He did exist, everything else also existed, [and thus He did not create the world out of nothing].

By resting on Shabbos we remember that G-d created the world out of nothing. For when everyone rests on one day of the week, people will notice and ask, "Why are you resting?" Our answer is, "*It was during the six weekdays that Hashem made the heaven, the earth, the sea and all that is in them, but He rested on Shabbos* (*Shemos* 20:11). This strengthens and bolsters everyone in the true faith.

Aside from remembering that the world was created out of nothing, [resting on Shabbos] also commemorates the miracle of the exodus from Egypt. We were slaves there, unable to rest when we wanted, but G-d rescued us from their hand and commanded us to rest on Shabbos. Therefore, the Torah mentions this in *sefer Devarim* as a second reason for resting [on Shabbos]. *You must remember that you were slaves in Egypt, when Hashem your G-d brought you out with a strong hand and an outstretched arm. Therefore Hashem your G-d commanded you to keep the Shabbos* (*Devarim* 5:15).

MITZVAH 33 ~ מצוה לג

TO HONOR ONE'S FATHER AND MOTHER

[I]t is a mitzvah] to honor one's father and mother, as it says, *Honor your father and mother* (*Shemos* 20:12). The Rabbis [in the Gemara] explain: What is meant by honoring? Providing them with food and drink, clothing and cover, and leading them in and out.

One ought to recognize anyone who was kind to him, treating him with kindness likewise. He should not be ungrateful, behaving like a stranger [toward his benefactor]. This is an evil character trait, utterly despised by G-d and man. When one is mindful that his father and mother are the cause of his existence, he will strive to give them every honor and render them any assistance, since they brought him into the world and worked hard for him when he was young.

Being grateful [to one's parents] brings one to recognize G-d's goodness, for He is the primary Cause of all mankind's existence since Adam Harishon. [He will realize] that G-d brought him forth into the light of day, providing for him all his life, bringing him to maturation hale and hardy in all his limbs, and endowing him with a thinking, rational mind. Indeed, if not for the intellect that G-d bestowed on him, he would be like a horse, like a mule without comprehension. He will then conclude how important it is to serve G-d.

MITZVAH 40 ~ מ מצוה

NOT TO BUILD AN ALTAR
FROM CUT STONE

———◦◦◦———

[The Torah forbids] building an altar out of stones touched by a metal [tool], as it says, *Do not build it out of cut stone* (*Shemos* 20). Cut stone refers to stone hewn with iron tools. An altar built from cut stones, is unfit for use.

We must realize that [the altar] from its inception brings forgiveness of sin, ultimately bringing blessing and peace. We were therefore commanded not to make [the altar] with iron tools which cut and are designed for destruction and bloodshed.

Since a person's character is affected by what he does and thinks, it is fitting that our actions in building the altar reflect the idea [of the altar.]

MITZVAH 42 ~ מצוה מב

THE JEWISH SLAVE

———◦◉◦———

[I]t is a mitzvah to treat] a Jewish slave according to the law that says, *If you buy a Hebrew slave, he shall serve for six years, but in the seventh year he is set free without liability* (*Shemos* 21:2). We must treat a slave as we are commanded, including setting him free in the seventh year [of servitude], or before the end of the seventh year, if the *yovel* year[3] occurred during that time . . . as our Sages derived from the Torah verses.

G-d wants Yisrael, His chosen people, to be a holy people, filled and crowned with every good and admirable quality, for thereby they will receive blessing. Kindness and compassion are among the most praised qualities in the world. Therefore we were commanded to have mercy on someone under our control, treating him with kindness, as it says in the Torah here and in the Oral Torah.

---

3 *Yovel*, the jubilee year, is the year at the end of seven cycles of shemittah (Sabbatical years) when all property is returned to its original owner and Jewish slaves are set free.

MITZVAH 50 ~ מצוה נ

PUNISHMENT OF DEATH BY THE SWORD

———◦○◦———

We are commanded to put one who transgresses certain commandments of the Torah to death by the sword. Our Sages of blessed memory call this [form of execution] slaying. This is considered an easy death, though strangulation is even easier. Included in this decree is a person who strikes his slave, even a non-Jewish slave, so that he dies by his hand, as it says, *[the death] must be avenged* (*Shemos* 21:20). [The Gemara] explains that the one who struck is put to death by the sword.

G-d wants to eliminate wickedness and brutality from the hearts of His holy people. Therefore, [the Torah] commands that anyone seized by anger so ferocious that he beats his vulnerable servant in his home to death, should be put to death. Although the servant is his property, and he lost his own property with [the servant's] death, nevertheless, he is slain for allowing his rage to overpower him to such an extent. This is a fitting and correct [death] sentence. *The judgments of Hashem are just, righteous altogether* (*Tehillim* 19:10).

MITZVAH 62 ~ מצוה סב

NOT TO ALLOW A SORCERER TO LIVE

————◈————

[W]e are commanded] to put to death a sorceress, as it
says, *Do not allow a sorceress to live* (*Shemos* 22:17).
This refers to anyone who practices witchcraft. The Torah
speaks in terms of what is typical, and more women practice
black magic than men.

Witchcraft is very harmful, bringing a great deal of misfortune on
people. I need not elaborate on this, since these things are known.
Therefore, we are commanded to remove anyone who engages in
sorcery from the world. The sorcerer acts against the wishes of
Hashem who wants [the world] to run by the laws of nature that
were established at the beginning of Creation. The [sorcerer] tries
to overturn everything.

To my mind, this is the concept of sorcery: At Creation,
Hashem, may He be blessed, established the laws of nature so
everything in the world could function in a useful manner for the
good of mankind. He ordained each creature to fulfill its task according to its species. Thus it says about all living beings, *after its
kind* (*Bereishis* 1:12). Furthermore, He appointed a heavenly force
over each [living being] to compel it to do its task, as the Sages
said, "There is not a blade of grass down on earth that does not
have a guardian angel above commanding it, 'Grow!'"

In addition to the regular assignment which each [living being]
fulfills by its nature, they can also function by one species mingling
with another species. This mingling has certain features that humans are not permitted to make use of, for G-d knows that these

functions can harm mankind. For this reason He restrained man from using them.

Based on this, the Sages stated a general rule: Whatever has therapeutic value is not considered "the way of the Amorites" and is not forbidden even if it contains traces of sorcery. Because it has a tried and proven benefit, it is not included in the forbidden features [of mingling species]. They were forbidden only because of the harm they cause.

Furthermore, the combining of [two species] was forbidden because it has the power to create something new. This power is so forceful that it temporarily voids the power of the guardian angel that is in charge of the two species. It may be compared to someone grafting one species onto a different one, creating a third species which is new. By grafting, he has nullified the power of both species.

Therefore, we are forbidden from even entertaining the idea, let alone doing with our hands, anything to change the perfect work of G-d. Perhaps this can help us understand the prohibition against mingling species of seeds, species of animals, and the wearing of *shaatneiz*.[4]

This is why the Sages said, "Why are the sorcerers called *keshafim*?[5] Because they diminish the power of the angels on high." They meant that their power is temporarily stronger than the power of the angels assigned to guard over [a species].[6] Notice how carefully the Sages chose their words, saying, "the angels on high" and not "the decree [issued] above," for Hashem ordained from the beginning of Creation that this should be the outcome of the mingling of two [species], proving conclusively that the [beings] appointed over the species [are only guardian angels]. Nevertheless the Sages said, the power of the guardian angels was diminished.

One whose mind is close to the radiance of the King and whose merit is above the guardian angels will have no fear of the actions of the sorcerers.

---

4 A mixture of wool and linen.
5 The word *keshafim* is seen as a contraction of *kachash, pamalia, ma'alah*— "weakening the power of the heavenly retinue [of angels]."
6 Each species has a guardian angel that supervises its growth. When two species are intermingled to form a new species, the two angels who guarded the original species are nullified as they have no control over the new strain.

MITZVAH 63 ~ מצוה סג

NOT TO MISTREAT A CONVERT

————◦◉◦————

[T]his mitzvah] forbids abusing a convert, even verbally. It is forbidden to disdain a non-Jew who converted to our faith, even with words, as it says, *Do not mistreat a convert* (*Shemos* 22:20). Even though we were already warned against mistreating a Jew, and one who converts to our faith is a full-fledged Jew, the Torah adds this warning about him, and even repeats it, saying, *When a convert comes to live in your land, do not hurt his feelings* (*Vayikra* 19:33). This is because emotional abuse is more painful to a convert than to a Jew [from birth], since a Jew [from birth] has champions to defend him.

Another reason for this prohibition is to keep [the convert] from backsliding to his former false ways out of anger over the insults he suffers. Thus it says in *Midrash Sifra*: Do not say to him, "Yesterday you were worshipping idols, and now you have entered under the wings of the *Shechinah*."

We must subdue our evil impulses. Therefore, the Torah cautions us about this vulnerable man who has no one to help him or depend on, stressing to us, since we have the power to hurt him, that we may not abuse him, even with words. Rather, we should treat him as one of our own. By restraining ourselves in this manner we will acquire a precious and exalted soul, adorned with virtuous qualities, worthy of receiving all good things. Thereby Hashem's desire to bestow goodness is fulfilled through us.

MITZVAH 65 ~ מצוה סה

NOT TO MISTREAT WIDOWS OR ORPHANS

———◦◉◦———

[T]his mitzvah] forbids oppressing orphans and widows by deed or word, as it says, *Do not mistreat a widow or an orphan* (*Shemos* 22:21). All our dealings with them should be conducted in a gentle, kind, and considerate manner.

[Widows and orphans] are helpless, since no one can argue their case as fervently as the widow's husband or the orphan's father would have done, were he alive. Therefore, our Torah commands us to be kind, compassionate, and honest in all our dealings [with them] as if their lawyer was arguing forcefully against us [on their behalf.] Let us pity them and treat them with compassion, pleading their cause even more [ardently] than their father [or husband] would have done had he been alive.

The Sages did say it is permitted to hurt orphans mildly for their own benefit. For example, a Rebbi teaching Torah, [or an instructor] teaching a vocation [is allowed to hurt him a bit.] Nevertheless, it is a mitzvah to be more lenient with them than with any other person.

Furthermore, [an orphan's] cry is answered by G-d, as it says, *If you mistreat them, and they cry out to Me, I will hear their cry* (*Shemos* 22:22). One is considered an orphan regarding this mitzvah until he no longer needs an adult to take care of his affairs.

MITZVAH 66 ~ מצוה סו

To Lend to the Poor

———◦◉◦———

[I]t is a mitzvah] to lend money to a poor man, in order to
bring him relief, easing his misery. The mitzvah of giving
a loan is greater than the mitzvah of giving *tzedakah*. If someone's poverty has become public knowledge and he is openly
asking for help, his distress is not as great as the person who
has not yet fallen to this level of shame and is fearful of it.
With the little help of a loan to tide him over, chances are he
will never ask for *tzedakah*. When G-d mercifully grants him
affluence, he will pay his creditors and live from the remain-
der.

G-d wants His nation to have the lofty qualities of kindness and
compassion. By training ourselves to acquire good character traits,
we become worthy to receive the [ultimate] goodness. As we have
said: Goodness and blessing are granted to good people, not to the
opposite. By bestowing goodness on good people, His wish is fulfilled, since His desire is to benefit the world.

Surely G-d could supply a poor man with everything he needs,
without us. It is only out of His kindness that He made us His
emissaries, [enabling us] to earn merit.

Additionally, G-d wants to sustain the poor man through the
help of human beings [as atonement] for his great sins. He is
pained in two ways: by suffering the disgrace of [accepting charity
from] his [successful] peers, and by being penniless.

MITZVAH 70 ~ מצוה ע

NOT TO CURSE HASHEM'S NAME

＝∞◎∞＝

Ｗe are forbidden to curse the Name of Hashem since this
evil utterance causes a person to become devoid of all
good; the splendor of his spirit becomes ruined, and he virtually
turns into an animal. In His kindness, Hashem distinguished
man from the animal world, and indeed he became man, with the
ability to speak. Now, with precisely that ability, he removes himself from rational thought, becoming like a loathsome, creeping animal. Therefore, the Torah warns us against this, because the good
G-d desires our well-being, and every utterance of ours that causes
[Him] to withhold His bounty, goes against His wish.

MITZVAH 71 ~ מצוה עא

Not To Curse a Leader

———◦◎◦———

[C]ursing a leader] is forbidden, as it says, *Do not curse a leader of your people* (*Shemos* 22:17). Though "*a leader*" refers to a king, the prohibition also includes [cursing] the *nassi* of Yisrael, namely, the head of the Great *Sanhedrin*, who was also the reigning leader. The Torah warns us about [cursing] anyone who is a leading figure in Yisrael, whether in the political arena or the realm of Torah.

It is impossible for a society to function without appointing one member as head, with others obeying his orders and carrying out his decrees. People always have different opinions, never unanimously agreeing on any one issue, resulting in deadlock and standstill. It is therefore necessary to accept the view of one person, for better or worse, so the needs of the community can be met. Sometimes his advice will be more successful than other times, but it is better than quarreling, which causes complete breakdown.

Since the appointed leader benefits the community, whether he is the leading [rabbi] guiding us in religious matters, or a political leader in charge of public safety, it is proper that we do not belittle his honor or curse him privately or publicly. For indulging in a bad habit privately, ultimately leads to public action, bringing about discord and its consequences.

MITZVAH 73 ~ מצוה עב

NOT TO EAT *TEREIFAH*

————◆◉◆————

[W]e are forbidden to eat *tereifah*] for it says, *Do not eat flesh torn off in the field by a predator* (*Shemos* 22:30). The verse warns us [against eating the flesh of] a domestic animal that was mangled by a wolf or lion in the field in such a way that it is likely to die from the lacerations. If [the predator] touched the tip of its ear or pulled out some wool it is not called *tereifah*. Rather our sages explain that [the animal] is torn to such an extent that it will soon die from its wounds. Our sages set the time at one year.

The soul uses the [human] body to carry out its task. Because the soul could never accomplish its duty without the body, it actually benefits from the body, instead of being hampered by it. Indeed, G-d never harms but only does good to benefit all. Thus we may say that the body is handled by the soul like a pair of tongs handled by a blacksmith; by using [the tongs] he forges useful objects.

If the tongs are strong and correctly shaped to grasp a piece of iron, the blacksmith can forge it into a functional object. But if the tongs are defective, the object that emerges will also be defective. Similarly, if the body is impaired, the mind is damaged likewise. Therefore our perfect Torah [told us] to stay far away from anything that causes defect to our bodies; and this is the simple reason the Torah bans forbidden foods.

Don't be surprised if some forbidden foods do not seem harmful to us or to the medical professionals. The faithful [divine] Physician who prohibited them is wiser than you and the [physicians]. How foolish to think nothing is harmful or beneficial, unless one understands why it is so.

It is for our own good that the reasons and the harm [of the forbidden foods] were not revealed. People who consider themselves wise might delude themselves into saying, "The harm the Torah says exists in that thing applies only in that location because such is its nature, or only to a person of such-and-such race." Because a fool may be swayed by their claims, the Torah did not reveal the reason, helping us avoid this stumbling block.

MITZVAH 74 ~ מצוה עד

NOT TO LISTEN TO A LITIGANT
IN HIS OPPONENT'S ABSENCE

————◈————

A judge is forbidden to hear the argument of one litigant
in the absence of his opponent, as it says, *Do not accept
a false report* (*Shemos* 23:1). People might lie when their opponent is not there, therefore the judge is warned about this so
he will not be influenced by such falsehood. This admonition
is also addressed to the litigant: He may not present his side of
the case to the judge when his opponent is not there, even if
the judge is willing to listen [to his arguments]. About this the
Torah says, *Keep away from anything false* (*Shemos* 23:7).

In addition, the Sages said this injunction is addressed to
anyone who tells evil tales, to anyone who listens to them, and
to a person who gives false testimony.

Falsehood is despised and abhorred by everyone; there is nothing
more loathsome than this, and any house that loves falsehood is
cursed, for Hashem is a G-d of truth, and everything about Him is
true. Blessing is only showered on those who emulate Him in their
deeds: being truthful, just as He is a G-d of truth, being compassionate just as He is compassionate, and doing acts of kindness, just
as He is abundant in kindness. But if one is a liar, his deeds are the
antithesis of G-d's attribute of truth, and the opposite of G-d's attributes will follow him forever. Since the opposite of G-d's attribute of blessing is damnation and curse; and the opposite of

41

G-d's gladness and peace is worry, quarreling, and distress, these will come from G-d to a wicked man.

For this reason the Torah warns us to keep far away from false-hood, as it says, *Keep distantly away from anything false* (*Shemos* 23:7). Because of the utter loathsomeness [of falsehood], the Torah uses an expression of *distance* a word not used in any other admonition.

Furthermore, we are warned against listening to anything sus-pected of being falsehood, even if we are not sure the particular matter is a lie. This is in line with what our Sages said: Keep far away from nastiness and the like.

MITZVAH 76 ~ מצוה עו

NOT TO FOLLOW A NARROW MAJORITY IN CAPITAL CASES

⁓◦◉◦⁓

[The Torah forbids] a presiding judge [in capital cases] to follow the majority, if the majority consists of only one man. When the judges disagree on the verdict, with some in favor of imposing the death sentence, and some against it, if those in favor [of the death penalty] outnumber those against it by one, the presiding judge may not condemn the accused to death, for it says, *Do not follow the majority to do evil* (*Shemos* 23:2). This means: Do not follow the majority that would impose a death sentence, for the intent of the phrase, *to do evil*, is to condemn to death. This law only applies when there is a narrow majority, that is to say, a majority of only one man. But when there is a majority of two, we decide the case on their word even to do evil [i.e., to condemn to death].

We are commanded to emulate the attributes of the Holy One, blessed be He, and one of His attributes is His abundant kindness, not dealing with people according to the strict letter of the law. We too, were commanded about this: in capital cases innocence should outweigh guilt because once a death sentence is carried out it cannot be reversed.

MITZVAH 77 ~ עז מצוה

Not to Blindly Follow the Opinion of a Senior Judge

———⊷◉⊷———

Ajudge should not blindly follow the opinion of a senior
judge, or even the majority opinion, to decide on the
guilt or innocence of [the defendant], without clearly understanding the case in his own mind, as it says, *Do not speak up in
a trial to incline yourself to follow the consensus* (*Shemos* 23:2).
This means, "Do not comment on a dispute if you are merely
following the opinion of a senior judge or the majority, but
you yourself don't understand it

This prohibition includes the rule that a defending judge
may not change his mind to argue for the prosecution, as it
says, *Do not speak up in a trial to incline* to prosecute, after you
have already argued for acquittal.

A judge should not accept his colleagues' opinion, without understanding the case himself, because this may cause a verdict to be
based entirely on the opinion of one [judge]; and Hashem did not
want a man's life decided on one person's opinion.

We are not worried about this concerning monetary disputes,
since that verdict can be overturned [and restitution made.] In fact
[a monetary dispute] need only be handled by a *beis din* of three,
relying on the fact that at least one of them is learned.

MITZVAH 78 ~ עח מצוה

To Follow the Majority

———◆———

[T]he Torah commands us] to follow the majority when the Sages differ about any law in the Torah, or regarding a legal dispute between two individuals. If some judges in a city find a man guilty, and some find him innocent, the majority must always be followed, as it says, *A case must be decided on the basis of a majority* (*Shemos* 23:2). The Sages commented: To follow the majority, is a Torah law.

When the wisdom of the two groups is equivalent, the opinion of the majority rather than that of the minority will agree with the truth. Regardless of whether or not one agrees with the majority opinion, the law dictates that we not deviate from their decision.

If we kept the Torah according to our own ability to understand its true intention, every Jew would say, "In my opinion this is the true interpretation of this matter." Even if everyone thought otherwise, he would have no right to act contrary to the truth as he interprets it. The result would be catastrophic—the Torah would splinter into countless Torahs, everyone judging according to his limited intelligence. But since we were explicitly commanded to accept the view of the majority, we have one Torah for all of us, guaranteeing our enduring existence. When we follow the dictates of the majority we fulfill G-d's commandment. Even if at times [the majority of] the sages err, it is they who are responsible, not us.

MITZVAH 84 ~ מצוה פד

To Observe Shemittah

——— ◉ ———

[T]he Torah commands us] to make all the produce of the land ownerless in the seventh year. [The seventh year] is called "the year of *shemittah*." Whoever desires the produce of the seventh year, may come and get it, as it says, *During the seventh year you must leave it alone and withdraw from it. The needy among you will then be able to eat [from your fields] just as you do, and what is left over will be eaten by wild animals. This also applies to your vineyard and your olive grove (Shemos 23:11).*

This mitzvah affirms in our hearts and minds the belief that the world was created out of nothing, *for in six days G-d made heaven and earth and he rested on the seventh day (Shemos 20:11).* Since He created nothing on the seventh day, He described Himself as resting. To eliminate the [false] concept that the world had no beginning and always existed, which those who deny the Torah and tear down its foundations and break its walls believe, we are obligated to devote our time, day after day, year after year, to this matter, by counting six years and resting in the seventh. By so doing, the matter never leaves our minds, just as we work six days of the week and rest on the seventh.

Besides not working the fields in the seventh year, G-d also commanded us to declare all the produce of the field ownerless, to remember that the fruit is not produced because of the fertile [soil], rather, there is a Master over the land and over [the farmer] who owns it, and at His will, He tells him to leave [the fruits] owner-less.

Another benefit gained from [observing *shemittah*], is acquiring the ability to forgo [for others]. There is no one as generous as one who gives without hope of being repaid.

Yet another benefit [from this mitzvah,] is that one strengthens one's trust in Hashem. Whoever relinquishes the fruit of an entire year, which he grew on his land that he inherited from his father, to the public, will become trained in this attribute for all his life. Neither miserliness nor a weakening of trust in G-d will ever trouble him or his family.

MITZVAH 87 ~ מצוה פז

NOT TO LEAD B'NEI YISRAEL ASTRAY

───────◦◉◦───────

The Torah forbids a person to urge others to worship idols. Even if he himself does not worship [the idol] or perform any [idolatrous] act, except for inviting [people], he is called, "one who leads astray." Our Sages expounded, *You must not let it be heard through your mouth* (*Shemos* 23:13), is a warning for one who leads others astray.

The admonitions to keep far away from idol worship and the extreme punishment for it are mentioned forty-two times in the Torah. The Torah also describes Hashem as vengefully jealous toward idol worshippers. The vengeful jealousy of G-d and the instructions to stay away [from idolatry] were written only to warn the worshippers. Surely, Hashem's glory does not increase nor diminish in the slightest whether human beings worship Him, an angel, a constellation, a star, or any one of His creations. The supreme degree of His glory and splendor is not subject to increase or decrease by anything, and certainly not through physical human beings who are His creations.

These punishments are to be understood from the perspective of those who receive from Him. When one removes himself from faith in Hashem, directing his body and thoughts to foolishness, he will be unworthy of any blessing or goodness. He will only be fit to receive the opposite of blessing, namely, curse, damnation, affliction, and all evil, since he is utterly removed from the domain of goodness and nothing but evil can reach him from all sides. By way of analogy, it is as if Hashem, who is the Master of goodness, became his enemy, blocking all goodness from reaching him. It is as if G-d is vengeful against him, for abandoning His worship and worshipping others.

However, G-d is not hostile or vengeful toward anyone. He has the power to [destroy] all of them, returning them along with the rest of the world to primordial emptiness by desiring their destruction, just as He created them by desiring their creation. G-d is only called vengeful in a figurative way, for the offender is punished in the way humans punish when they become angry and vengeful.

MITZVAH 88 ~ מצוה פח

THE *CHAGIGAH* OFFERING

———◦◉◦———

[I]t is a mitzvah] to celebrate the three Yamim Tovim, by going up to the Beis Hamikdash three times a year—shortly before Pesach, Shavuos, and Sukkos, to celebrate the [Yamim Tovim] there, as it says, *Offer a sacrifice to Me, three times each year* (*Shemos* 23:14). We must bring an animal sacrifice there as a peace-offering in honor of the Yom Tov. This mitzvah is repeated twice in the Torah.[7] Our Sages taught: Yisrael were given three mitzvos regarding the three *Yamim Tovim*: bringing a *chagigah* offering, bringing the Yom Tov offering, and rejoicing.[8]

It is not proper to come empty-handed before G-d. Even though He needs nothing from us, as it says, *Even if I were hungry, I would not tell you, for Mine is the whole world and its fullness* (*Tehillim* 50:12), we must imagine we are standing before Him. People are closer to the Beneficent One in the Beis Hamikdash, than in any other place, and the light of the King's countenance shines on them there. Therefore, it is fitting for us to bring the offering at this time. By bringing the offering we become ready to receive goodness and our souls are uplifted, as we will write with the help of Hashem.

---

7   *Shemos* 23:24, *Devarim* 16:16.
8   The joy of Yom Tov was expressed by enjoying a meal of *shelamin* (peace offering]. If the offerings brought in fulfillment of vows, free-will gifts, or as tithe were not enough for all participants, additional *shelamim* had to be brought as *shalmei simchah*, offerings of rejoicing (Rashi).

MITZVAH 91 ~ מצוה צא

TO BRING THE FIRST-FRUITS

[I]t is a mitzvah] to bring *bikkurim* to the Beis Hamikdash. [*Bikkurim*] are the first fruits that ripen on a tree. We are required to bring them there, giving them to a kohen. Not all trees are included in this mitzvah by Torah law, only the seven kinds for which Eretz Yisrael is praised, namely: wheat, barley, grapes, figs, pomegranates, olives, and dates, as it says, *Bring your first fruits to the House of Hashem your G-d (Shemos* 23:19). The Oral Torah explains that this only refers to these seven fruits.

This mitzvah focuses our thoughts on Hashem while we are in great joy, reminding us that He is the source of all our worldly blessings. For this reason we were commanded to bring the first of the fruit that ripens on His trees to [the kohanim,] the servants of His House. By accepting His sovereignty and giving thanks to Him when we recognize that these fruits and all other good things come from Him, we become worthy of blessing. Thus our harvest will be blessed.

MITZVAH 95 ~ מצוה צה

TO BUILD THE BEIS HAMIKDASH

⚬⚬⚬

[I]t is a mitzvah] to build a House for the sake of Hashem. This means we bring our offerings there, we make pilgrimage there on the [three] Yamim Tovim, and it is the gathering place for all Yisrael every year. As it says, *They will make Me a sanctuary* (*Shemos* 25:8). This mitzvah also includes [making] the utensils that are needed for the service in the Beis Hamikdash, such as the *menorah,* the table, the altar, and the other articles.

My son, Hashem wants us to fulfill the mitzvos because He wants to benefit us. By doing the mitzvos, man becomes worthy and ready to receive His good, thereby Hashem bestows goodness on him. He therefore revealed to Yisrael the path to become virtuous. This is the path of the Torah, for through it man becomes virtuous. Whoever fulfills His mitzvos makes himself eligible to receive His goodness, thus fulfilling His desire. Conversely, whoever does not prepare himself is acting badly, since He knows that Hashem desires [to bestow goodness on him,] yet he acts in ways that preclude Him from fulfilling His desire.

A portion in the Torah is written for the sole purpose of teaching us this basic idea. It is found in *parashas Eikev: And now Yisrael, what does Hashem want of you? Only that you remain in awe of Hashem your G-d, so that you will follow all His paths and love Him, serving Hashem your G-d with all your heart and with all your soul. You must keep Hashem's commandments and decrees that I am prescribing for you today, so that goodness will be yours* (*Devarim* 10:12,13). In other words, G-d asks nothing from you when you observe the mitzvos, except that in His great goodness He wants to do you good. In the next verse it says, *The heaven, the heaven of heaven, the earth and everything in it, all belong to Hashem* (ibid. 10:14)—implying, He does not need your mitzvos, however out of His love for you, [He wants] to benefit you.

Having established the significance of the mitzvos, we add that building a Beis Hamikdash for Hashem in which to offer prayers and sacrifices to Him is intended to prepare our hearts for His service. He does not need to dwell in a house built by people nor to shelter in their roof, even if it were built of the cedars of Lebanon or of cypress wood. Heaven and the heaven of heaven cannot contain Him, as they endure by His spirit, much less does His glory need a house built by man, G-d forbid. It is obvious that its purpose is to make our bodies acceptable [for blessing]. For the body becomes fit [to receive blessing] through its actions. The more good deeds one performs continuously, the more the thoughts of his heart are purified, cleansed, and refined.

Hashem desires goodness for man, therefore He commanded us to establish a place that would be absolutely pure and clean, where people can purify their thoughts, directing their hearts toward Him. Perhaps Hashem chose that place, because it is the center of the world, and the center is preferred to the extremes, or perhaps for some other reason known to Him. Through the merit of our deeds and the purity of our thoughts in that place, our intellect attains fellowship with Divine wisdom.

Along these lines, we can also explain the purpose of the sacrifices. Since man's heart is influenced by his actions, he cannot achieve atonement for his sins by declaring privately that he sinned and will henceforth refrain from sinning. He must do an impressive act, such as taking a fattened sheep from his flock and toil to bring it to the kohanim in the House of Hashem where it will be offered in the prescribed manner. Through this impressive act he will realize the wickedness of his sin and will refrain from sinning in the future.

The words of the Ramban are similar. He explains that the sacrifices can be understood on a simple level as follows: Since man's
deeds are carried out through thought, speech, and action, G-d
commanded that a man should lay his hands on his sin offering,
[for laying hands] represents action. He confesses his sin verbally
which represents speech, and the innards and the kidneys, which
are the instruments of thought and desire, are burnt. The legs,
which correspond to man's hands and feet with which he works,
are also burnt. The blood is sprinkled on the altar because his
blood gives him life; he will thereby realize that he sinned against
G-d with his body and soul, deserving that his blood be spilled and
his body burned, were it not for the kindness of the Creator, Who
accepts this offering as exchange and ransom. The animal's blood
takes the place of his blood, and its life is instead of his life. The
main limbs and organs of the offering parallel his limbs and organs,
and portions [of the sin-offering] are eaten by the kohanim in
order to sustain the teachers of the Torah so they will pray for him.
The reason for the daily public offering is to help the public continually avoid sin. These words are easy to grasp and appealing to
the heart like all Aggadah teachings.

We may explain further, that we were commanded to always
bring sacrifices from things that man desires in his heart such as
meat, wine and bread, so that his heart will be deeply inspired when
bringing them. The poor man too, brings his offering from the bit
of flour which his eyes and heart are focused on all day.

Additionally, the heart is more inspired by animal sacrifices because they are comparable to man's physical body in every way except that man has intelligence and the animal does not. Since the
only difference between man and an animal is his intellect, when he
sins not using his intellect, he becomes exactly like an animal.
Therefore he was commanded to take the flesh of an animal which
is just like his flesh, bring it to [the Beis Hamikdash,] the place chosen for the elevation of the intellect, and burn it there until it is totally burnt and forgotten, instead of his own body.

Thereby man will realize that everything relating to his body
without his intellect is worthless, and he will rejoice with the intel-

ligent soul G-d has granted him which lasts forever. Even the body that is associated with [the intellect] will merit eternal life at the revival of the dead if it follows [the intellect's] advice, guarding against sin. If one sets this idea firmly in his mind, he will surely avoid sin. The Torah assures us that through this great deed [of bringing an offering] and regretting his sin wholeheartedly, one's inadvertent sin will be forgiven. However, for deliberate sins, this analogy [between the human and animal body] is not enough to bring forgiveness. The intentional sinner is not castigated by analogies and words, [rather by punishment with] *a rod for the back of fools* (*Mishlei* 26:3). . . .

MITZVAH 97 ~ מצוה צז

To Arrange the Showbread

———◦◉◦———

[I]t is a Torah command] to place showbread continually in the Beis Hamikdash, as it says, *It is on this table that showbread shall be placed before Me at all times* (*Shemos* 25:30).

Man is sustained on bread which needs continual blessing. By occupying ourselves with Hashem's mitzvah [performed with bread,] His will and blessing will bring blessing on our food, since a person is blessed with whatever he uses to do the will of G-d. The wellspring of blessing will flow to him in accordance with his thoughts and actions when he does a mitzvah.

Our Sages taught a similar lesson: [G-d says,] "Bring an *omer* on Pesach before Me, so your produce in the fields may be blessed. Bring two loaves on Shavuos before Me, so the fruit of your trees may be blessed. Pour your libation water on Sukkos, so the rains of the year will be blessed. Sound the shofar [on Rosh Hashanah] before Me, to recall the binding of Yitzchak."

The Sages said that since the showbread was used for a mitzvah, and through it the will of G-d was done, it contained great blessing. Every kohen who received a portion, even as small as a bean, was satiated.

MITZVAH 99 ~ מצוה צט

THE PRIESTLY GARMENTS

———◦◦◦———

The kohanim were commanded to wear special clothing for glory and honor when performing the service in the Beis Hamikdash, as it says, *Make holy garments for Aharon and his sons* (*Shemos* 28:4).

A person is influenced by his actions, and his thoughts and intentions are motivated [by his deeds]. [The kohen,] who is the agent to bring atonement, must focus all his thoughts and intention on the service [he is performing]. Therefore he wears specially designed garments for [the service], so that he will be deeply aroused and reminded of [the One] in whose Presence he is serving when he gazes at any part of his body. This is similar to the mitzvah of wearing *tefillin* which everyone places on his body as a reminder to be virtuous. Although the kohen also wore *tefillin*, because of the importance of his post he needed [special garments] as well.

Additionally, the kohen wears special garments to enhance the honor of the Beis Hamikdash and its service. We have already written that as the glory and awe of the Beis Hamikdash are strengthened, the hearts of sinners will be softened, inspiring them to return to Hashem.

NOT TO OFFER LEAVEN OR HONEY
ON THE ALTAR

————⊷◈⊶————

[T]he Torah prohibits] offering leaven or honey on the altar, as it says, *For you may not burn any leaven or honey as a fire offering to G-d* (*Vayikra* 2:11). The prohibition is repeated at the beginning of the verse where it says, *Do not make any meal offering that is sacrificed to Hashem out of leavened dough* (ibid.).

Though the reasons for this mitzvah are obscure, my intention to offer reasons [for the mitzvos] is to teach young people that the words of the Torah have reason and purpose. Thus from the start they will accept the mitzvos according to their level of comprehension. They will not consider the mitzvos as words of a sealed book, and although they are young, they will not rebel against them, chasing after foolishness. Therefore I will write something that comes to mind at first glance. Realizing this, no critic should attack me for any reason.

An offering stirs the thoughts of the person who brings it, and his action will make an impression on his soul. *Chameitz* takes a long time [to rise.] By keeping it far away from his offering, a person will infer that he should adopt the trait of alacrity in doing G-d's will. As the Sages said, "Be light as an eagle, swift as a deer, and strong as a lion, to do the will of your Father in heaven." This is necessary for the *minchah*-offering of an individual rather than

58

the *minchah*-offering of the community, for gloom and listlessness are more prevalent in an individual, since people in a community will caution each other [against succumbing to lethargy]. Therefore the Torah did not object [to the use of *chameitz*] for a *minchah* of the community that was brought occasionally, such as the two loaves on *Shavuos*.

To satisfy the young children, we can explain that the use of honey is excluded [from an offering on the altar,] as a lesson that one should refrain from pursuing sweets, [and not be] like gluttons and drunkards who are always drawn to sweet things. They will train themselves to select only foods that are healthful and nutritious, as every intelligent person should do. A bright person understands that mere physical gratification is shameful; surely one should not take more pleasure in physical acts other than what is absolutely necessary. One of the great thinkers wrote that our sense of touch is shameful for us.

I heard another reason for the prohibition against *chameitz* and honey. Leaven inflates itself, and honey likewise expands when boiled. Thus, they were banned because they represent one who is haughty as it says, *Every haughty heart is an abomination to Hashem* (*Mishlei* 15:5).

MITZVAH 119 ~ מצוה קיט

TO SALT ALL OFFERINGS

[I]t is a Torah command] to offer salt on all offerings. One must place salt on the meat of an [animal] sacrifice, and likewise on the flour of a meal-offering, as it says, *You must offer salt with all your offerings* (*Vayikra* 2:13).

The mitzvah of offerings makes the one bringing them noble and upright. Therefore, man was commanded to offer good and savory food which he relishes, to arouse himself. Similarly, salt is [added], so the act [of sacrifice] will lack nothing and be in keeping with the conventional life style of people, for food without salt is tasteless and unappealing. Thus, his soul will be stimulated.

Furthermore, salt preserves everything, preventing spoilage and decay. So too, bringing an offering saves a person from [spiritual] downfall, protecting his soul so it will live forever.

MITZVAH 120 ~ מצוה קכ

THE OFFERING FOR AN ERRONEOUS RULING

‒‒‒◆‒‒‒

The Great Sanhedrin must bring an offering if [the judges] mistakenly ruled against *halachah,* regarding serious sins punishable by *kareis*—excision or premature death— and the community or its greater part acted on their word, as it says, *If the entire community of Yisrael commits an inadvertent [violation] as a result of [the truth] being hidden from the [the Sanhedrin, who are the] congregation's eyes* (*Vayikra* 4:13).

An offering subdues man's lustful tendency, heightening his intellectual aspirations. Obviously, an error made by the great [Torah scholars] is due to a weakness in their intellect. Since their intellect needs strengthening, they must come to the Beis Hamikdash, where an abundant flow of [divine] intelligence is hovering. They will bring an offering there, which will bring them to realize the baseness of the carnal impulse which caused their error, and to recognize the nobility of straight and pure thinking. These pure thoughts will put them on guard to act wisely in their future rulings.

MITZVAH 124 ~ מצוה קכד

NOT TO SEVER THE HEAD OF
THE SIN OFFERING BIRD

————◦◦◦————

W hen the kohen brings a bird as a sin-offering, [the Torah forbids him] to separate the head of the bird from its body when he performs the *melikah*, as it says, *He shall gouge through the neck from the back without separating [the head from the body]* (*Vayikra* 5:8).

With *melikah*, the kohen digs his fingernail into the nape of the bird's neck at the neck-bone [instead of the usual *shechitah* slaughtering, in which the windpipe and gullet are cut from the front of the neck with a knife]. He cuts through the bone with his fingernail until he reaches the windpipe and gullet. He also cuts them, or at least the greater part of one of them, with his fingernail. This constitutes the *shechitah* for a bird brought as a sin-offering. The kohen must be careful not to cut so far that the head is severed from the body, for it says explicitly, *without separating [the head from the body]*.

Possibly, *melikah* is done by the hand of the kohen on the bird brought as a sin-offering, because this offering is brought by a poor man [who cannot afford to offer a sheep]. This hints that one should rush as fast as he can [to supply] the poor man's needs. [The poor man's] offering does not require *shechitah*, so the kohen need not look for a knife and check it, keeping the poor man away from his job. To speed up the process, [G-d] also ordained that the kohen start at the nape of the neck [of the bird] since it is close at hand, and he will not have to turn its neck to the side facing the windpipe and gullet.

There is another symbolism in the *melikah* procedure which severs the nape of the neck of turtle doves and young pigeons. It urges the Jewish people who are compared to [these birds] not to be stiff-necked.

The prohibition against severing the head from the body completely, enhances the offering, for leaving the head attached to the body [of the bird] makes the offering more glorious, and we do all we can to make a poor man's offering as dignified as possible. It is hard enough for him that he is poor; we need not add to his plight by diminishing the appearance of his offering.

By offering sacrifices to Hashem, we adopt good and noble qualities, purifying our actions with proper intent. Since man is a physical being, his soul is strongly affected by his physical activities. Until we hear another reason we will stay with this one.

MITZVAH 132 ~ מצוה קלב

To Light Fire on the Altar

[I]t is a mitzvah] to keep a fire continuously burning on the altar every day, as it says, *There shall be a constant fire kept burning on the altar* (*Vayikra* 6:6). The sages interpreted this to mean putting wood on the altar every morning and evening. Our Sages explained that although fire descended from heaven, it was a mitzvah to bring natural fire.

Don't ask, "Since they were commanded to burn the sacrificial offerings, which could not be done without fire, why do we need this mitzvah?" This is a separate mitzvah. In fact they burned a separate fire on the altar specifically for this mitzvah, in addition to the fire needed for the offerings.

It is well-known, that G-d in His great goodness, performs major miracles for mankind in hidden ways, so the events seem to happen in natural ways. Even about the celebrated miracle of the splitting of the Red Sea, it says, *During the entire night, Hashem drove back the sea with a powerful east wind, transforming the sea bed into dry land, and the waters were divided* (*Shemos* 14:21). Intelligent people understand that concealment is necessary because of the lofty state of G-d, and the lowly state of the people for whom the miracle is performed [who would not be able to endure the impact of an open miracle].

Therefore, G-d commanded us to burn fire on the altar even though fire also descended from heaven, in order to conceal the miracle. For this reason the fire from heaven was not visible on its descent, with three exceptions: The fire of the eighth day of the inauguration [of the *Mishkan*] (*Vayikra* 9:24); the fire of Gid'on (*Shoftim* 6:21); and the fire of Mano'ach (ibid. 13:20).

Man is blessed through the actions he performs for his Creator. Because blessing spreads through similar mediums, the bread he needs for sustenance is blessed through his service of the showbreads. So too, man's fires will be blessed through performing service to G-d with fire. This explains the necessity of an additional fire besides the fire used to burn the offerings.

What is man's fire? Man's natural ability to live and act. Of the four elements[9] in man, fire is the dominant one, since it strengthens man, enabling him to move and function. Therefore [fire] needs blessing more [than the other elements]. The goal of blessing is to achieve completion, with nothing missing or anything superfluous. The fire in man needs this blessing, so man should have the correct amount of fire. He should not have less, or his strength will be weakened, and too much would burn him. People die from fever which is an excess of fire.

The sons of Aharon added fire without being commanded to do so (*Vayikra* 10:1), therefore, their internal fire was increased, and they were burnt. A person receives punishment or blessing, corresponding to his actions.

---

9   Earth, air, fire, and water

MITZVAH 143 ~ מצוה קמג

To Burn the Remnants of Kodashim

───◈───

I t is a mitzvah to burn *nosar*, the meat of the holy offerings left over after the allotted time for eating them has expired. For it says, *What is left over from the sacrifice's flesh on the third day must be burned in fire* (*Vayikra* 7:17). This burning is a positive mitzvah.

Leftover meat spoils, developing a stench. Therefore, out of respect for the offering, Hashem commanded us to burn it immediately, removing it from the world, so people will not be disgusted by its smell.

The best method for utter destruction is achieved with fire, rather than by grinding it into small pieces to scatter in the wind, or other methods.

This mitzvah also hints that one should trust in Hashem, not skimping on his food to save it for the next day, since he sees that G-d utterly destroys sacred meat once its time has passed, not allowing any creature, neither man nor animal, to have any benefit from it.

MITZVAH 151 ~ מצוה קנא

Not to Leave the Sanctuary
During the Service

The kohanim may not leave the sanctuary during the service, as it says, *Do not leave the entrance of the Communion Tent lest you die* (*Vayikra* 10:7). This prohibition is repeated for the *kohen Gadol,* as it says, *He may not leave the sanctuary* (*Vayikra* 21:12).

We should exalt the glory of the Beis Hamikdash and its services. Therefore one should not go out, turning his back on the precious service for anything. By leaving the service, he humiliates it, for by casting it aside even momentarily for something else, he shows there is something greater than the service of Hashem. Therefore we are warned against this with the penalty of death.

THE EIGHT UNCLEAN ANIMALS

[T]he Torah ordained] that eight smaller animals are unclean, causing defilement, as it says, *These are the smaller animals that creep on the land which are unclean to you: the
weasel, the mouse, the ferret . . . (Vayikra 11:29).*

There is no man who can attain total knowledge, so that nothing
is hidden from him. Even about Moshe, the Sages said, "There are
fifty gates of wisdom; all were given to Moshe, except for one."
Similarly, King Shelomoh said about himself, *I thought I could become wise, but it is beyond me (Koheles 7:23).* No sensible person
doubts that Hashem is the Father and Source of all wisdom, which
is totally contained in Him; and that the Father of all goodness only
commands His creatures for their own benefit and well-being, in
order to save them from harm.

When we realize the benefit we derive from the mitzvos, let us
rejoice in that. And when we cannot understand the benefit of a
particular mitzvah, we must realize that Hashem in His infinite wisdom commanded us to do so, knowing the benefit we will gain
from that mitzvah.

Our Sages explain that we do not know the reason for all the
mitzvos, because knowing the reasons might bring about our
downfall. Indeed, [the reason] for two [mitzvos] were revealed,

and [King Shelomoh] a great man of the world, was devastated through them.[10]

Knowing that the wisdom of G-d is greater than any wisdom, and that He commands us only for our benefit, we should have no difficulty with any forbidden food or law of uncleanness, even if the benefit cannot be understood, for truthfully, everything is for our good.

Therefore, my son, do not wonder about the laws of ritual impurity, though the reason is deeply hidden from the understanding of human beings; possibly this impurity is harmful to the soul, weakening it slightly. Our Sages taught that the phrase, "*because it will make you impure*" (*Vayikra* 11:43)—can be read *it will make you stopped up*. The wellsprings of intelligence within the enduring soul become clogged by ritual impurity.

Intelligence is affected by physical matters, because not withstanding their differences, the soul is linked to the body.

How can mere mortals, who are incapable of understanding the soul and its nature, understand through research and analysis what ails and cures the soul. Even physicians cannot find a remedy until they understand the underlying makeup of the sickness. Therefore, we cannot grasp the basis for the laws of ritual defilement until we attain knowledge of the soul, its nature, its origin, and its aim.

Knowing this, you will realize that we will always question the underlying reasons for the mitzvos of ritual defilement and purity, and there will almost be a veil over our face [precluding us from understanding] the laws of the red cow, which defiles the clean and purifies the unclean.

---

10 The Torah gives the reason for the prohibition against a king marrying many wives because they will lead him astray, and the reason he should not acquire many horses because this will lead him to return to Egypt. Thinking that in his wisdom he would be immune to these temptations, Shelomoh violated these laws with tragic repercussions.

MITZVAH 169 ~ מצוה קסט

THE IMPURITY OF A *METZORA*

————◦◎◦————

I t is a mitzvah for a person stricken with *tzaraas*[11] to come ask the kohen about his *tzaraas*. The kohen will declare him either ritually pure or impure, and instruct him accordingly. He must not consider this a natural illness; rather he must realize it is the result of the gravity of his sin, as it says, *If a person has a blotch, discoloration, or spot on his skin . . . he shall be brought to Aharon, or to one of his descendants who are the kohanim* (*Vayikra* 13:2).

Hashem, with open eyes, oversees each person individually, observing all his deeds, as it says, *For [His] eyes are upon man's ways, and He sees all his steps* (*Iyov* 34:21). Therefore, He warned us to take this evil sickness to heart, reflecting on the fact that it was caused by sin, rather than by chance. The Sages explain that [*tzaraas*] is most often the result of evil tale mongering. We show [this disease] to the kohen, a person who administers atonement to sinners. This association helps the sinner reflect on repentance. He is quarantined for a few days, enabling him to examine his actions unhurriedly. He may be required a second quarantine, possibly because he repented halfheartedly. A second quarantine will cause

---

11 Tzaraas is a form of leprosy which afflicts one who transgressed certain sins. He must go to the kohen who declares him pure or impure. At times he orders him to be quarantined until we are able to discern if he is in fact impure. Once it is established that he is impure, he must live separated from other people.

him to repent fully, becoming pure. These quarantines manifest Hashem's individual supervision of each person.

Because there are many opinions regarding how Hashem oversees His creations, there are many verses and mitzvos to teach us this fundamental principle.

Some people believe that Hashem's Providence is on everything in the world; no living being or object moves at all without His will and command. A leaf only falls from a tree because it was preordained to do so, and it was impossible for it to fall a second sooner or later. This opinion seems far removed from the intellect.

Some evil scoffers opine that Hashem oversees neither humans nor any living thing in this lowly world. This is the evil and bitter opinion of the scoffers.

We, who believe in the true faith, affirm that G-d's watchful care extends over all living creatures in general. Every species in the world will endure forever;[12] never perishing entirely, through His Providence. However, we believe that His providential individual supervision is reserved for the human species, and it is He *who comprehends all their deeds* (*Tehillim* 33:15). We received this [doctrine] from our great Sages, and there are many verses proving it.

Therefore, when *tzaraas* strikes a man, he must immediately realize it was caused by his sins and avoid social gatherings like a man who is shunned for his evil deeds, associating only with [the kohen], who will atone and heal the injury of sin. By showing the kohen his affliction, and by listening to [the kohen's] advice, and through self-examination, the affliction will depart, for G-d who watches over him constantly, will see his repentance and heal him. This is the reason for the quarantine, as we have said.

---

12 Although it seems that there once existed animals that are now extinct, our sages tell us that there were species that were destroyed at the time of the Flood. It is also possible that some of the extinct animals are from the same species of animals which still exist. Ed.

MITZVAH 170 ~ מצוה קע

NOT TO SHAVE THE HAIR OF A *NESEK*[13]

———◆———

[T]he Torah forbids] shaving the hair on a *nesek*, as it says, *[The person] shall shave himself, without shaving the nesek* (*Vayikra* 33:15). Thus, the kohen will be able to discern the signs of impurity in the hair.

Every man should bear the pain and punishment Hashem decrees on him, without complaining. He must realize that he is unable to conceal his punishment from people and he can only beg G-d to heal him.

---

[13] A nesek is a type of tzaraas affliction in the hair.

MITZVAH 171 ~ מצוה קעא

RULES OF CONDUCT FOR A METZORA

———◆———

Aperson with *tzaraas* must follow the rules outlined in the Torah, as it says, *[As long as the affliction is upon him it shall make him impure and he shall be impure, he must sit alone, outside of the camp shall be his dwelling. (Vayikra 13:46)] His clothing must be torn, he must go without a haircut, and he must cover his head down to his lips* (ibid 13:45). It also says, *"Unclean! Unclean! he must call out* (ibid.), which means indicating with his body that he is *tamei,* so others avoid him. All people who are *tamei* must identify themselves thus.

By being ostracized, the person will conclude that sin causes one to be banned from all good, and he will turn back from his evil ways. Our Sages put it this way, "With his evil gossip he caused a rift between man and his wife and between man and his fellow; therefore, let his tent be outside the camp [away from the community]." It is therefore fitting that he call out [that he is *tamei*], so everyone will turn away from him.

One is judged by the same scale he himself judged. This does not mean, G-d forbid, that Hashem judges people in accord with the good or evil He receives. Hashem has only everlasting goodness, kindness, and mercy. In every season and in every hour His mercy is ready for everyone who is fit to receive it. *The guardian of Yisrael neither slumbers nor sleeps (Tehillim* 121:4). The Sages meant that a man's actions cause him to receive payment. Whatever

73

a person does causes him to be blessed in kind, or punished.

Man punishes himself when he strays from the path of righteousness, by making himself unfit to accept goodness. This can be compared to one who travels on a straight path, cleared from stones and pitfalls, with walls of thorns on either side. If he veers from the path and hurts himself, we cannot say Hashem wanted to hurt this person; rather he hurt himself by not walking carefully. So too, when one sins, we cannot say Hashem wanted to punish him, rather his sins made him unworthy of good and he becomes susceptible to punishment. And so our sages said, "No evil comes from Above.

When bad things happen to a person, it is because G-d hides His face from him. Because of his sin, G-d removes His protection from him, so he receives the punishment he deserves. Afterwards, He will command His angels to guard him as before. As it says, *I will hide My face from them, and they will be their enemies' prey. Beset by many evils and troubles, they will say, "It is because my G-d is no longer with me that these evil have befallen us (Devarim* 31:17)."

A learned scholar wrote: We know that Hashem is One; change only comes through the recipients [of reward and punishment]. Hashem does not change His deeds, for they are all done with wisdom.

MITZVAH 173 ~ מצוה קעג

THE PURIFICATION OF THE METZORA

———◆———

I t is a mitzvah for a metzora to purify himself, his garment, or his house, using wood of a cedar tree, hyssop, a red thread, two birds, and flowing water, as prescribed in the Torah.

Perhaps immersing in water purifies an impure person so that a man will consider himself newly created at that moment—just as the newly created world was entirely water, as it says, *G-d's spirit moved on the water's surface* (*Bereishis* 1:2). Just as his body is renewed, so will he resolve to renew his behavior and mend his ways, doing good deeds and carefully observing the ways of Hashem.

For this reason the Sages prohibited purification with water in a vessel. Only spring water or collected well water that is in the ground is permissible, because it appears in his mind as the world made entirely of water, helping one to see himself emerging from it as a new person. A person cannot imagine this mental image if the water is in a vessel, for there is a limit to the contents of a man-made vessel. He will not visualize the vessel as the primordial world of water, and he will not see himself becoming a new person at that moment.

You may accept or reject this explanation.

MITZVAH 174 ~ מצוה קעד

To Shave the Metzora
at his Purification

⟨⟩

T he *metzora* shaves his hair to complete the second stage
of purification, as it says, *On the seventh day, he shall shave
all his hair* (*Vayikra* 14:9).

The Torah wanted the person to feel as though he were created
today with his hair just beginning to grow, and make a new start.
Just as he is shaved clean from all his hair, he can be cleansed thoroughly of all stains. He should purify his body zealously and vigor-
ously to emerge from the uncleanness of his *tzaraas*. By doing so,
he will also cleanse his deeds, turning them from bad to good,
making them meritorious.

MITZVAH 216 ~ מצוה רטז

NOT TO HARVEST THE EDGE OF ONE'S FIELD

———⋙◉⋘———

[I]t is a mitzvah] to leave over the edge of one's field [for the poor], as it says, *Do not completely harvest the end of your field. Leave them for the poor and the stranger* (*Vayikra* 19:9,10).

A person must leave over some produce at the edge of the field when he harvests his crop. The Torah does not specify how much to leave, however, the Sages set a minimal amount of one sixtieth.

Hashem wants the people He chose, to be crowned with every good and precious quality, having a blessed soul and a generous spirit. I have written previously that one's soul is influenced by his actions. Thus [through his good deeds his soul] becomes good, and the blessing of Hashem can be conferred on him. By leaving part of the produce of his field ownerless to benefit the needy, [the farmer] senses an inner satisfaction, gaining an upright and blessed spirit. He will feel Hashem satisfying him with His goodness, and his soul will repose in goodness. But one who gathers his entire crop in his house, leaving nothing for the poor despite their hunger and desire for the grain, displays an evil heart and a wicked character. [In retribution,] evil will befall him. As the Sages said, "A person is measured by the scale with which he measures."

MITZVAH 231 ~ מצוה רלא

NOT TO CURSE A JEW

———◦◉◦———

[T]he Torah prohibits] cursing a Jew, whether man or woman, even if he does not hear the curse, as it says, *Do not curse the deaf* (*Vayikra* 19:14). [The Sages] explain this to mean one who does not hear your curse.

We do not know how a curse affects the one who is cursed, nor what force there is in speech; but most people, whether Jewish or not, are afraid of curses, saying that even the curse of an ordinary person leaves a mark, affecting the cursed person with curse and pain.

Hashem restrains us from causing harm to others with our speech, just as we are restrained from harming others by our actions. The Sages said, "A covenant was made with the lips," meaning, a man's words make an impact.

Man's power of speech has a spiritual source, as it says, *He breathed into his nostrils the soul of life, and man became a living spirit* (*Bereishis* 2:7), which Onkelos translates as, "a talking spirit." Perhaps that is why [speech] was given great power to act even on things removed from it. We know and see that the more saintly and righteous a person is, the faster his words take effect. This is widely recognized among the wise and learned [scholars].

Perhaps [this prohibition] is designed to end friction among people, causing them to live in peace, for *a bird of heaven will carry the voice* (*Koheles* 10:20), and the curse might reach the ears of the one he cursed [which will ignite hatred and contention].

The Rambam of blessed memory, wrote that this mitzvah prevents the one who wishes to curse from anger and vengeance. He apparently felt that the curse does not cause actual harm to the one who was cursed; the Torah prohibits it only so people will not be accustomed to revenge, anger and lowly character traits. We will accept the interpretation of all our teachers, although my heart inclines toward my interpretation.

MITZVAH 241 ~ מצוה רמא

NOT TO TAKE REVENGE

———◦◦◦———

The Torah forbids taking revenge. If a Jew harmed someone in any way, although most people would not rest
until they paid him back in kind for his evil deed, Hashem restrains us from doing this by saying, *Do not take vengeance*
(*Vayikra* 18:18).

The Midrash expounds: How do we define revenge? One
asked another, "Lend me your sickle," and the other does not
lend it to him. The next day the other asks him, "Lend me
your axe," and he replies, "I will not lend it to you, just as you
did not lend me your sickle." About this it says, *Do not take revenge*. This applies in all similar cases.

One should know and internalize that whatever happens to him,
good or bad, is brought about by Hashem. Even if another person
is the agent, nothing can happen unless Hashem wills it. Therefore,
if someone hurts you, realize that your bad deeds are the cause, and
Hashem decreed this to happen. Do not retaliate, for the tormen-
tor is not the primary cause of your trouble; your sin brought it on.
As David said [when Shim'i ben Geira cursed him], *He is cursing
because Hashem said to him, "Curse David,"* (2 *Shemuel* 16:10). He
ascribed the matter to his sin, not to Shim'i ben Geira.

Additionally, this mitzvah prevents quarreling, removing hate
from people's hearts. Once there is peace among men, Hashem will
bring peace to them.

MITZVAH 244 ~ מצוה רמד

Not to Crossbreed Livestock

———◦◉◦———

[T]he Torah forbids] the crossbreeding of two species of animals. We may not couple an animal with any domestic or wild animal that is not of its species, as it says, *Do not crossbreed your livestock with other species* (*Vayikra* 19:19).

Hashem created His world with wisdom, understanding, and knowledge, making each form according to its needs to further the destiny of the world, as set by Hashem. Thus it says regarding Creation, *G-d saw all that He had made, and it was very good* (*Bereishis* 1:31). *G-d saw*, means His knowledge and understanding of things. In His lofty greatness, G-d does not need to see things after they have been created, since everything is revealed and visible to Him before the thing is made.

But the Torah speaks to people in words they can understand, attributing to Hashem things familiar to man, since a human being only grasps concepts he is acquainted with. Which man can understand something beyond his comprehension? The Sages used the phrase, "in order to make the ear accept what it is able to grasp."

Since G-d created everything perfectly adapted to the purpose it must fulfill in the world, He commanded each and every species to produce offspring of its own kind, as it says in *parashas Bereishis*. The species may not intermingle, lest they fall short in perfection, and He will not bestow His blessing on them. Therefore, we are forbidden to mate different species of animals.

MITZVAH 247 ~ מצוה רמז

The Fruit of the Fourth Year

———⊙⊙⊙———

[The Torah decrees] that the fruit of the fourth year is entirely holy. All fruit growing on a tree in its fourth year since planting, must be eaten in Yerushalayim by its owner like the second tithe; this is its holiness, as it says, *When you plant any tree bearing edible [fruit] . . . In the fourth year all [the tree's] fruit shall be holy, and it shall be something for which Hashem is praised* (*Vayikra* 19:23,24). The Rabbis explain that [the fruit] belongs to the owner, and the words *Hashem is praised* implies that he eats it in Yerushalayim.

G-d wanted man to praise Hashem with the first and choice fruits of his trees, which are those that grow in the fourth year, so that Hashem's blessing will rest on him and his fruit. Since the beneficent G-d desires good for His creatures, He commanded us to take [the fruit] up [to Yerushalayim,] eating it in the site He chose for His worship, *For there Hashem has commanded His blessing* (*Tehillim* 133:3).

Furthermore, since the teachers of Torah and wisdom reside in Yerushalayim, if a man will eat the fruits there, he will be inspired to set up his home or his children's homes there to learn Torah.

MITZVAH 248 ~ מצוה רמח

To Eat and Drink in Moderation

⟨◉⟩

[The Torah warns us] not to overindulge in eating and drinking in our early years. The Sages expound on this in connection with the "stubborn and rebellious son" (*Devarim* 21:18).

Most sins are committed because of excessive eating and drinking, as it says, *Yeshurun became fat and rebelled, you grew fat, thick, and gross, and abandoned the G-d who made it* (*Devarim* 32:15). And so our Sages said, "Who made you rebel against Me? The horse-beans I gave you to eat." They also coined the phrase, "A full stomach leads to sin."

Food is fuel for the body, whereas contemplation of abstract ideas and the fear of G-d and His mitzvos, is food for the soul. Because the soul and body are diametrically opposed, as the food of the body increases, the nourishment of the soul decreases. For this reason some Sages never ate more food than was necessary to stay alive, as it says, *A righteous person eats to satisfy his soul* (*Mishlei* 13:25).

The perfect Torah, for our own good, restrains us from overindulging in food and drink, to prevent man's physical side from overpowering his spiritual aspect, ultimately weakening and destroying it completely.

MITZVAH 249 ~ מצוה רמט

OMENS AND SUPERSTITIONS

———⊙———

[T]he Torah forbids] us to act on the basis of omens, as it says, *Do not act on the basis of omens* (*Vayikra* 19:26). This is repeated elsewhere, *Among you there shall not be found anyone who divines by omens* (*Devarim* 18:10).

These things are utter insanity and nonsense, and it is not fitting for G-d's chosen nation to pay attention to such lies. Moreover, they cause one to stray from belief in Hashem and His holy Torah, enticing him to complete rejection [of Judaism]. He will attribute anything that happens to him to chance and coincidence, rather than to G-d's close supervision, thus forsaking all fundamental principles of the Jewish faith.

Hashem commanded us to believe that all evil and good come from the One Above, according to our deeds. Omens neither help nor harm us, as it says, *No black magic can be effective against Yaakov and no occult powers against Yisrael* (*Bamidbar* 23:23).

MITZVAH 250 ~ מצוה רנ

NOT TO FOLLOW AUSPICIOUS TIMES
AND MAGIC

[The Torah prohibits] acting on the basis of auspicious times, as it says, *Do not act on the basis of auspicious times* (*Vayikra* 19:26). *Midrash Sifra* explains: We must not say as the phony fortune-tellers say, "This hour is good for doing this particular project, and one who does it then will be successful, whereas one who does it at another time will fail."

Our Sages included optical illusions that people perform, in this prohibition. This talent combines sleight of hand and lightning speed, which make people think the magician is performing supernatural feats. He may put a rope in his garment, and pull out a snake. Or he may throw a ring in the air and then pull it from the mouth of someone in the audience, and many such tricks.

The reasoning behind this law is similar to the prohibition against acting on the basis of omens. Additionally, women and young boys will accept as reality thing that are actually impossible. Their minds will be trained to accept the impossible, without understanding it as a miracle from the Creator. This can cause them to deny the fundamental principles [of Judaism,] and their souls will be cut off [from life in the hereafter].

NOT TO COMMUNICATE WITH THE DEAD

———— ◆◈◆ ————

[T]he Torah prohibits] the practice of *Ov*, or asking anything of an *Ov*, as it says, *Do not turn to Ovos* (*Vayikra*
19:31). The [*Ov*] practitioners burned incense and did things
which caused one to imagine hearing a voice emanating from
the [practitioner's] armpit, which answered questions.

Similar to the prohibition of acting on the basis of omens, this
causes a person to leave the true faith and turn to foolishness, believing that everything happens by chance. He will try to improve
his lot and remove every harm from himself, by asking [the *ov*]
questions, and [believing in] the antics he performs. But this will
not help him, because everything is decreed by the Master of the
universe, and his fortune will change according to his virtuous or
sinful deeds, as it says, *For He repays the deeds of man, and causes
man to find according to his conduct* (*Iyov* 34:11).

This is the ideology of every upright Jew. Moreover, the practice
of the *Ov* and the magician involve an element of idolatry.

MITZVAH 257 ~ מצוה רנז

TO HONOR TORAH SCHOLARS

⸻⸻

[I]t is a mitzvah] to honor Torah scholars, and rise before them, as it says, *Stand up for a white head* (*Vayikra* 19:32), which Onkelos translates as, "Rise before one who studies Torah." [The verse continues,] *and show respect for an old man.* The Sages explained that *an old man* refers to one who has acquired wisdom.

The Torah describes a Torah scholar as *an old man*, because a young Torah scholar perceives with his wisdom what an old man knows through [the experience of] many years.

Man's purpose in this world is to acquire wisdom, to recognize his Creator. By honoring one who has attained this wisdom, others will be encouraged to [attain it as well.] In the Gemara in *Kiddushin,* Issi ben Yehudah explains that even an unlearned old man is included in this mitzvah, because over the course of his long life, he has recognized some of the deeds and wonders of Hashem and for that he deserves honor. Rabbi Yochanan ruled that the *halachah* is according to Issi ben Yehudah. However, this applies only if [the old man] is not a habitual sinner; for if he is, he forfeits that honor.

MITZVAH 263 ~ מצוה רסג

LAWS OF KOHANIM

————◦◉◦————

A kohen may not defile himself by contact with the dead, except for his relatives mentioned in the text, as it says, *Let no kohen defile himself to a soul among his people* (*Vayikra* 21:1). Even though the soul of a good person does not die, the verse applies the word "soul" to the body, because [the soul] is the purpose of the body.

Kohanim were chosen for the service of Hashem, as it says, *They shall be holy to their G-d* (*Vayikra* 21:1). He therefore detached them from [contact with] the dead. Ritual impurity is loathsome, and the Sages call the impurity of a dead man "the father of fathers of impurity", meaning a corpse conveys a higher degree of impurity than any other source of impurity.

When a person's intellect leaves, he remains a mere pile of empty, worthless flesh, eager to do wicked things. In fact, the body's evil character caused the precious soul to sin while it dwelled in it. Therefore, it makes sense, that [a corpse] which is the corporeal substance stripped of its glorious soul, defiles everything around it.

Thus [the kohanim], who are servants of Hashem, must stay away from [all corpses], except the blood relatives that the Torah permitted to them. All the ways of the Torah are pleasant, and its paths are peace. Since the kohanim might be disturbed if they could not approach the tent of close relatives who died to soothe

88

their spirit by weeping for him, the Torah permitted them to do so.

The words of the Sages seem to confirm this, since they said the remains of perfect tzaddikim do not cause impurity. Since their body was pure, not causing their soul to sin, rather it helped it gain merit, their soul departs with a "kiss of G-d," while a light hovers over their body forever.

MITZVAH 264 ~ מצוה רסד

LAWS OF MOURNING

———◈———

Akohen must defile himself by coming in contact with
the [deceased] relatives mentioned in the Torah, as it
says, *For her [i.e., his deceased unmarried sister] he must defile
himself* (*Vayikra* 21:3). This is a positive mitzvah as expounded in *Sifra*: *For her he must defile himself*—this is a mitzvah; if
he does not wish to defile himself, he is defiled against his will.

Man is influenced by his actions. Being physical by nature, man is
only influenced by something actual. When a close relative whom
he naturally loves, dies, the Torah requires him to take specific actions which cause him to concentrate his thoughts on his grief, so
that he will realize that his sins were the cause. For He does not
torment capriciously nor afflict man,[14] except for sin. This is the
firm belief of the precious Jewish faith. During the days of mourning, a person will do *teshuvah*, improving his conduct as best he
can. Thus the mitzvah of mourning has great benefit for man.

---

[14] *Eichah* 3:33

NOT TO SLAUGHTER AN ANIMAL
WITH ITS YOUNG

———◦◦◦◦———

[T]he Torah forbids] slaughtering an animal and its young on the same day, whether they are consecrated or non-holy, as it says, *Do not slaughter a [female animal] and its child on the same day* (*Vayikra* 22:28).

G-d exercises a general supervision over all living beings, which guarantees the survival of all species. No species will become totally extinct as long as the world exists.

Although His supervision over mankind is directed at each individual, this is not the case with other species of living creatures. Rather, Hashem watches over each species generally. We are forbidden to [slaughter a mother together with her child] which is like destroying the tree together with its branches, to hint at this idea.

In addition, this implants within us the trait of pity and removes from us the evil trait of cruelty. Although G-d permitted [slaughtering] living animals for our sustenance, He commanded us not to kill a mother and her young together [on the same day], to etch the trait of compassion firmly in our consciousness.

MITZVAH 298 ~ מצוה חצר

PESACH

———◆———

[T]he Torah] prohibits us from working on the first day of Pesach, the 15th of Nissan, as it says, *The first day shall be a sacred holiday for you when you may not do any service work* (*Vayikra* 23:7).

The Jewish people must remember the great miracles Hashem performed for them and their ancestors. They must talk about them, and tell their children and grandchildren about them. By resting from worldly concerns, they have time to involve themselves with these ideas. Even light work preoccupies people, causing the glory of Yom Tov to be forgotten.

Another benefit of resting [on Yom Tov] is that the people have the opportunity to gather in synagogues and houses of study and listen to lectures on Scripture. The [spiritual] leaders of the community give guidance and teach wisdom, as the Sages said, "Moshe instituted that Yisrael teach the laws of Pesach on Pesach and the laws of Shavuos on Shavuos."

TO COUNT THE OMER

[T]he Torah commands us] to count forty-nine days from the day of the bringing of the *omer*, which is the sixteenth of Nissan, as it says, *You shall count seven complete weeks following the [Pesach] holiday when you brought the omer as a wave offering* (*Vayikra* 23:15).

This counting is mandatory. We count each day, and each week, because the verse says, *you shall count fifty days,* and also, *Count seven weeks for yourself* (*Devarim* 23:15). Expounding on this subject in the Gemara *Menachos,* Abbaye said: It is a mitzvah to count the days, and a mitzvah to count the weeks.

The raison d'être for the existence of the Jewish people is the Torah. Heaven, earth, and the Jewish people were created only because of the Torah, as it says, *If My covenant with the day and with the night would not be, I would not have set up the laws of heaven and earth* (*Yirmeyah* 33:25).

Thus, the purpose of Yisrael's redemption and exodus from Egypt, was to receive the Torah at Sinai, as Hashem said to Moshe, *Proof that I have sent you, will come when you take the people out of Egypt. All of you will then become G-d's servants on this mountain* (*Shemos* 2:12). The verse means, "Your [act of] taking them out of Egypt will be a sign for you that you will serve G-d on this mountain." You will receive the Torah, which is the primary purpose for their redemption; this is the supreme good for them, surpassing their liberation from bondage. Hashem made their release from slavery a sign for Moshe of their [impending] acceptance of the Torah, since the less important matter becomes a sign for the matter of greater importance.

Because Torah is the reason for Yisrael's existence and for their redemption and rise to eminence, we were commanded to count the days from the second day of Pesach until the day of the Giving of the Torah; showing how deeply we yearn for this day. This is like a slave who looks forward to liberty, constantly calculating when the longed-for day of freedom will arrive. Counting [the days] shows that a person's dreams are focused on that desire.

MITZVAH 311 ~ מצוה שיא

ROSH HASHANAH

———◦◉◦———

[T]he Torah prohibits us] from working on the first day of Tishri, as it says, *The first day of the seventh month shall be a day of rest for you . . . Do not do any service work [on that day]* (*Vayikra* 23:25).

On this day, mankind is judged for their deeds. G-d surveys the deeds of every individual, not in a general way, rather all human beings metaphorically pass before Him single file, to be judged one by one.

Because of G-d's love for humanity, He surveys their deeds one day each year, so their sins do not accumulate, and thereby the prospect for atonement exists. In His abundant kindness G-d tips [the scales of justice] toward the side of kindness, and if [the sins] are few in number, He ignores them. If there are sins that require cleansing, He exacts payment for them in small installments. Our Sages said in the same vein, "One collects a debt from a loved one bit by bit." Were G-d to delay demanding payment, [the sins] would accumulate and the world would deserve destruction, G-d forbid.

This revered day, which guarantees the existence of the world, should be a Yom Tov. However, since it is a day of judgment for everyone, we behave with more awe and fear than on the other Yamim Tovim. This is the reason for the mitzvah of sounding the shofar of remembrance. The broken staccato sound of the *teruah*, reminds everyone to break the force of his evil impulse and regret his bad deeds.

MITZVAH 313 ~ מצוה שיג

YOM KIPPUR

———◦◉◦———

[T]he Torah commands us] to fast on the tenth day of Tishri which is Yom Kippur, the Day of Atonement, as it says, *The tenth day of this seventh month . . . you must afflict yourselves* (*Vayikra* 23:27). The Midrash in *Sifra* explains that affliction means causing a decline of vitality, thus we abstain from eating and drinking. Our Sages also forbid washing, anointing, wearing shoes, and marital relations.

Out of His love for His people, Hashem established one day in the year to atone for their sins with *teshuvah*. We were commanded to fast on that day, because food and drink, and other delights of the senses arouse the body to lust and sin. This impedes the soul from seeking the truth, which includes the service of G-d and His ethical teachings, which are good and sweet to all intelligent people. On his day of judgment, a servant should not appear with a hazy and confused mind, dimmed by food, drink, and selfish thoughts of the physical world. For a man is judged based on his deeds at the time [of judgment]. Let him uplift his spiritual intellect and subdue his material impulse before that revered day, so he may be acceptable and ready to receive atonement, without the barrier of physical desires standing in the way.

MITZVAH 324 ~ מצוה שכד

THE FOUR SPECIES

———※◎◎◎※———

On the first day of Sukkos we take in our hands the fruit of a citron tree, a palm frond, myrtle branches, and willows, for it says, *On the first day you must take for yourselves the fruit of a beautiful tree, branches of a palm tree, branches of a thick tree, and willows of the brook* (*Vayikra* 23:40). The Rabbis explain that *the fruit of a beautiful tree* means an *esrog;* the *branches of a palm tree,* refers to a *lulav; branches of a thick tree* denotes the myrtle, and *willows of the brook* means the familiar willow branch.

Dear son, I have written many times that a person is influenced by the things which occupy him continually; his thoughts and outlook on life are shaped by his activities, good or bad. Therefore, wishing to confer merit on His chosen nation Yisrael, G-d gave them mitzvos in abundance so their character might be positively influenced, all day.

The mitzvah of *tefillin* which are placed against the organs of intellect, namely, the heart and the brain, direct our thoughts toward serving Him in purity. A person will focus his thoughts on [doing] good, remembering to aim for honesty and righteousness in all his doings [by putting on the *tefillin*].

The mitzvah of the *lulav* and its three species is similar. The Yom Tov is a time of great rejoicing for Yisrael, since the crops of the field and the fruit of the trees are gathered then. Thus, the Yom

Tov is called the Yom Tov of the Harvest. G-d commanded His nation to celebrate a Yom Tov before Him at this time, to confer merit on them by dedicating the primary objective of their rejoicing to Him.

Since joy arouses the animal nature of man, making him forget the awe of G-d, Hashem commanded us to take objects to remind us that our joy should be for His sake and His glory. These four species gladden the heart of those that behold them and are fitting reminders during this season of gladness.

Additionally, these four species hint to important organs within man. The *esrog*, alludes to the heart, the site of the intellect, hinting that one should serve G-d with his intelligence. The *lulav* parallels the spine, the backbone of man, suggesting that one should direct his body to serving G-d. The myrtle leaf connotes the eyes, implying that one should not stray after [the temptations of] his eyes on the day when his heart rejoices. The willow leaf stands for the lips, hinting that a person should guard what he says, demonstrating his awe of Hashem even when rejoicing.

MITZVAH 330 ~ מצוה של

THE YOVEL YEAR

[T]he Torah commands us] to count seven cycles of seven
years in Eretz Yisrael, until the *yovel* year, as it says,
*You shall count seven sabbatical years, that is, seven times seven
years* (*Vayikra* 25:8).

The mitzvah of counting the years of *shemittah* until the
yovel year was commanded to the Sanhedrin, the great *beis din*.
They counted each year, for seven cycles of seven years, until
the *yovel* year, just as we count the [forty nine] days of the
omer [day by day and week by week.] They consecrated the
fiftieth year by leaving the land fallow, proclaiming freedom
for all male and female [Jewish] servants, and returning all
land to the [original] owners.

Everything belongs to Hashem, and ultimately everything returns
to whomever He originally gave it. The earth is His, as it says, *For
the land is Mine* (*Vayikra* 25:23). This mitzvah helps people refrain
from stealing the land of their neighbor and from coveting it in
their hearts, since everything returns to the one G-d chooses.

This is similar to what earthly kings do. From time to time they
take land from their officers to keep them in awe of their masters.
So too, Hashem wants the lands to return to the one that He had
originally given it, and servants shall be released to return to the
domain of their Creator. However, earthly kings do this because
they are afraid that the officials might rebel against them, whereas

G-d, who desires with His great benevolence to benefit us, commanded us for our own good.

I heard from scholars that there is a profound secret regarding the yovel, which hints at the history of the world and its years. We count seven year cycles, not eight or nine year cycles, because this number has great significance. The cycle of seven is found in many mitzvos. We work six days and rest on the seventh; we work the land six years and rest on the seventh; after seven cycles of seven years we rest on the yovel year; Pesach is seven days as is Sukkos, which is followed by Shemini Atzeres. We count seven weeks from Pesach and afterwards is the holiday of Shavuos. Similarly, when making a covenant which represents permanence we use the number seven, as [Avraham said,] *these seven sheep you shall take from me [as testimony] (Bereishis 21:30)*. The wise Bilam also made seven altars.

MITZVAH 344 ~ מצוה שדמ

THE HEBREW SERVANT

———⟐———

We may not force a Hebrew servant to do the degrad-
ing and demeaning work of a Canaanite [pagan]
slave, for it says, *Do not work him like a slave* (*Vayikra* 24:39).
In *Midrash Sifra*, our Sages explain that [the Hebrew slave]
should not carry a *linta* behind the master. This small pillow
was carried by a slave for the master to sit on when he got
tired. In the same vein, the Rabbis said that the [The Hebrew
servant] should not carry his master's garments before him to
the bathhouse. We apply these [precedents] to similar cases.

This mitzvah makes us realize that our nation is the most honored
of all [nations], and we will come to love His nation and His Torah.
Furthermore, we will realize that just as this Hebrew servant was
sold because of his impoverishment, so too, someone may possibly
buy us or one of our sons if we sin. While treating one's servant
with respect, one will surely become aware of these thoughts, prod-
ding himself to be careful not to sin against Hashem.

Additionally, this mitzvah trains one to practice kindness and
compassion, and to stay away from the evil trait of cruelty. A person of good character is worthy of receiving good, and Hashem delights in showering His blessings on His people, as I have written
many times.

THE *CHEREM* OATH

[T]he law of *cherem*] is to be understood as follows: Whoever bans one of his possessions with a *cherem* oath, declaring, "This object of mine, shall be *cherem*," must give that object to the kohanim, as it says, *However, any banned property that a man will set aside for the sake of Hashem, ...shall be holy [going to the kohanim]* (*Vayikra* 27:28).

G-d chose Yisrael from all other nations to recognize His Name and serve Him. Unlike other nations, they are not under the dominion of the constellations [of the zodiac,] rather [they are guided] by the hand of the Holy One, blessed be He, as it says, *But His own nation remained Hashem's portion, Yaakov was the lot of His heritage* (*Devarim* 32:9). When He redeemed them from Egypt, a miracle that encompassed the entire nation, He Himself in His glory brought them out. As the Sages expounded in the Pesach Haggadah: *I will pass through Egypt on that night* (*Shemos* 12:12)— I, and not an angel; *and will kill every first-born in Egypt—I*, and not a *saraf*, etc.

When Yisrael clings to the Torah, adorning themselves with it, only goodness and an abundant flow of blessing descends on them, and a spirit of generosity and purity upholds them, while curse and ruin is their enemies' portion.

When a Jew becomes enraged, uttering a *cherem* curse on his assets and property which are in the blessed domain of Hashem, this mitzvah lets us know that it is impossible for him to remove them from that domain because Yisrael is the portion of Hashem, and whatever a servant acquires belongs to his master. However, since the intention of the one who pronounced the *cherem* was to remove that object from his possession, it is fitting to fulfill his intention by consecrating the object, thus returning it to the ownership of his Master.

MITZVAH 360 ~ מצוה שס

To Tithe Domestic Animals

———◦◦◦———

[T]he Torah commands us] to tithe all kosher domestic
animals. The tithe of cattle, sheep, and goats, born in
our herds each year, are taken to Yerushalayim and eaten there
after their fat and blood is offered on the altar, as it says, *All
tithes of the herds and the flock that are counted under the rod,
every tenth one shall being consecrated to Hashem* (*Vayikra*
27:32).

G-d chose Yisrael, and for the sake of their righteousness desired
that they all be engrossed in Torah and know His Name. Most people, driven by their base physical impulse, do not immerse themselves in Torah study. Therefore in His wisdom, He gave them the
opportunity to know the words of His Torah.

Each year, every herdsman brought the tithe of his herds to
Yerushalayim, the center of Torah and the seat of the Sanhedrin.
He also brought there the second tithe and the fruits of the fourth
year. Since one surely desires to dwell where he can access his resources, either he or one of his sons will move to Yerushalayim to
study Torah while being sustained by the produce [which must be
eaten in there].

Thus, every house in Yisrael would have a learned man, well-
versed in Torah to teach the household, and thereby, the land will
be full of knowledge of Hashem. Were there only one or a few
Torah scholars in a city, many men and certainly women and chil-

dren, would not have an opportunity to see him. Even were they to hear him speak once a week, this would not be reinforced in the home. But with a teacher in every house to constantly alert them, nothing sinful or inappropriate will occur. Thus they will deserve the blessing of, *I will keep My sanctuary in your midst . . . I will be a G-d to you, and you will be a nation [dedicated] to Me* (*Vayikra* 26:11,12).

MITZVAH 362 ~ מצוה שסב

To Purify the Camp

[T]he Torah commands us] to send people who are *tamei* [ritually unclean] out of the camp of the Divine Presence, as it says, *Instruct B'nei Yisrael to send out of the camp anyone who has tzara'as or a male discharge, and all who are tamei through the dead* (*Vayikra* 5:2). In the wilderness, the boundary of the camp of the *Shechinah* was obvious. In later generations the camp of the *Shechinah* referred to the area of the *Beis Hamikdash* and the courtyard facing it.

It is known to the wise, that *tum'ah* saps the strength of a man's soul, disconnecting it from [G-d's] perfect Higher Intelligence. It remains detached until he is cleansed, as it says about *tum'ah*, *Do not defile yourselves with them, because it will make you tamei* (*Vayikra* 1:43). Our Sages interpreted *it will make you tamei* to mean, "it will make you spiritually insensitive." In other words, the wellsprings of the intellect become clogged through *tum'ah*. It is not acceptable for a man soiled with *tum'ah* to be in [the Beis Hamikdash], the place of holiness and purity, where the spirit of G-d resides.

This may be compared to a king's palace; anyone with *tzaraas*, or who is loathsome in body or clothing is denied access. The same idea is expressed in the verse, *For it was forbidden to enter the king's gate in a garment of sackcloth* (*Esther* 4:2).

MITZVAH 364 ~ מצוה שסד

To Confess Sin

------~◊◊◊~------

[The Torah commands us] to confess to Hashem the sins we have committed, when we regret them. When one repents he must confess, saying, "I beg of You, Hashem, I have erred, been iniquitous, and willfully sinned before You, doing such and such." He explicitly articulates the sin he has committed, elaborating [on his wrongdoings] according to his eloquence, and pleads for forgiveness

By verbalizing his confession, the sinner demonstrates that he believes all his actions are known to G-d, and G-d's eye sees all. Additionally, by verbalizing the sin explicitly and being remorseful, he will be more careful not to transgress in the future. Thereby he will become cherished by his Creator.

TO GROW THE NAZIR'S HAIR

———※◎※———

[T]he Torah decreed] that a *nazir*—a man who separates himself from wine—is required to let his hair grow during the period he is a *nazir* to Hashem, as it says, *The uncut hair on his head shall grow* (*Bamidbar* 6:5). Midrash Mechilta expounds: *The uncut hair on his head shall grow*—is a positive mitzvah. How do we know it is also a negative mitzvah? Because it says, *No cutting instrument shall touch [the hair] on his head* (ibid.)

Our intellect is theoretically fit to stand before the Creator, recognizing His glory like one of the heavenly beings standing before Him. However, because Hashem desired that [the intellect] be encased in a physical lodging; it must occasionally cease serving the Creator to take care for the needs of his lodging [i.e., the body], for a house will not last unless man watches over it.

It's good for man's intellect to curtail its service of the physical [body] and strive to serve his Creator, as long as it does not neglect the housekeeping [of his body], destroying it. This would be a sin, since the King wants man to live through his body.

Indeed, Rabbi Yose said, "A person is not allowed to afflict himself by fasting." Rabbi Yehudah in the name of Rav derived this from the verse, *and man became a living soul* (*Bereishis* 2:7). The Torah means that we must actively keep our souls alive. Similarly, the wise king [Shelomoh] said, *Do not be overly righteous or excessively wise. Why be left desolate? (Koheles* 7:16).

The exalted holiness of the *nazir* is manifested by subduing his physical cravings but not destroying his body completely, for example, he abstains from wine and lets his hair grow. He controls his evil impulse, leaving his body unaffected. The function of his intellect is strengthened, and the glory of Hashem rests on him. Because the Divine service of his intellect is not diminished by [the demands] of his physical body, the purpose of Creation will be fulfilled in him.

Letting one's hair grow, subdues the evil impulse, as we find in the Gemara Nazir. Shimon Hatzaddik said: I never ate from the guilt offering brought by a *nazir*, except for one instance when a *nazir* came from the south. He was handsome, with beautiful eyes, and locks of hair set in curls. I asked him, "Why did you commit yourself to destroy your beautiful hair?"[15]

He replied, "I was a shepherd for my father. Once, when drawing water from the well, I gazed at my reflection in the water. At that moment, my evil impulse pounced, trying to drive me from this world. But I said to my lust, 'Evil creature! Why do you boastfully intrude into a world that is not yours? [You are proud of something] that is destined to become worms and maggots! I swear [that I will become a *nazir* and] shave off [this beautiful hair] for the sake of Heaven.'"

[Said Rabbi Shimon,] "I immediately rose and kissed his head, saying, 'My son, May there be many *nezirim* like you in Yisrael! The Torah had you in mind when it says, *When a man or woman expresses a nazirite vow to G-d (Bamidbar* 6:2).'"

---

15 At the end of the term of his vow, a *nazir* must shave off his hair.

MITZVAH 376 ~ מצוה שעו

Not to Defile a Nazir with a Corpse

———◦◦———

[T]he Torah decrees] that a *nazir* may not become *tamei* through contact with the dead, as it says, *He may not defile himself even when his father, mother, brother, or sister dies* (*Bamidbar* 6:7).

There are great stringencies imposed on a *nazir;* he is forbidden to become *tamei* even for his father or mother, although an ordinary kohen who is also sanctified, may become *tamei* for them.

The sanctity of a kohen is conferred on him automatically without his consent; he is sanctified by virtue of being born to his holy tribe. Regarding relationships, there is no difference between a kohen and anyone else, except that on occasion he serves in the Beis Hamikdash. He is at home with his loved ones, filled with warm feelings for them, and vice versa. He was therefore permitted to become *tamei* for them, for all the ways of the Torah are pleasant, and all its paths are peace.

By contrast, a *nazir* to Hashem, is holy to Hashem for the duration of his vow, as it says, *Since his G-d's nazirite crown is on his head* (*Bamidbar* 6:7). He does not become *tamei* by indulging in worldly delights, nor does he attend festive celebrations or family parties. By abstaining from wine he devotes himself to improving his soul, turning away from the coarse pleasures of the flesh. Focused on [elevating] his precious soul, and ignoring his physical needs, he no longer desires the company of friends and loved ones, except for the sake of a mitzvah. With his elevated spiritual level, his soul finds the delights of the body and the company of others meaningless. [His soul] only finds pleasure in the holy service [of G-d] to which it has committed itself.

Just as a *kohen gadol* is separated from his friends, and all his actions and thoughts are focused exclusively on the service of G-d, so too is the *nazir*. Therefore, the Torah forbids the *nazir* to become *tamei* for his family, just as *kohen gadol* is forbidden to [become *tamei* to his closest relatives]. However, oil is only mentioned in connection with the *kohen gadol*, since he was anointed with it, whereas oil is not mentioned by a *nazir*. About the *kohen gadol* it says, *Since his G-d's anointing oil is upon him* (*Vayikra* 21:12), whereas about the *nazir* it says, *Since G-d's nazirite crown is on his head* (*Bamidbar* 6:7).

You may ask, "Since a *nazir* returns to his youthful pursuits when his nazirite period is over, why should he be treated more stringently than an ordinary kohen?" We assume that a *nazir* will wish to continue consecrating himself, becoming more virtuous day by day, and Heaven will approve of his plan. The Sages said about this, "One who wishes to be cleansed, will be assisted by Heaven." In fact, having vowed to be a *nazir* even for one day, [Heaven] will help him, enabling him to live his life in purity.

MITZVAH 378 ~ מצוה שעח

THE PRIESTLY BLESSING

The kohanim were commanded to bless Yisrael every day, as it says, *This is how you must bless Yisrael* (*Bamidbar* 6:22).

Hashem, in His great goodness, wishes to bless His people through his servants who serve in the House of Hashem, committed to Him with awe all day, for through them blessing will descend on [Yisrael.] All their undertakings will be blessed, and the pleasant goodness of Hashem will rest upon them.

Don't ask, "If Hashem wants [Yisrael] to be blessed, why not grant the blessing Himself? Why is there need for the kohanim to bless them?" Our good deeds are the instruments that convey blessing to us. G-d's hand is open to anyone who asks, to the extent that he is worthy and fit to receive G-d's bounty.

Since He chose us out of all the nations wanting us to be worthy of earning His benevolence, He commanded us to act virtuously and elevate ourselves through His mitzvos. He commanded us to ask for blessing from Him, through His pure servants. This will bring merit on our souls, and thereby we will be worthy of His goodness.

MITZVAH 380 ~ מצוה שפ

The Second Pesach Offering

Whoever is unable to bring the Pesach offering on the fourteenth of Nissan because he is *tamei* or is on a faraway journey, should bring the Pesach offering on the fourteenth of Iyar, as it says, *He shall prepare it on the afternoon of the fourteenth of the second month (Bamidbar 9:11).* Our Sages taught that this applies not only to one who was *tamei* or on a faraway journey, but to anyone who did not bring the first Pesach offering, whether deliberately or not.

The Pesach offering is a powerful sign that the world was created out of nothing. For on Pesach, G-d performed great miracles and wonders for us, changing the [laws of] nature for all nations to see. All the nations of the world recognized that He supervises and governs the physical world. Thereby they realized, that He created the world out of nothing when He desired, at the date [of Creation]. Just as the laws of nature dictate that creating something from nothing is impossible, so too, it is impossible to divide the depths of the sea for a massive throng to walk across on dry land, and then return the sea to its place; and to sustain a great populace with food from heaven, day after day. All the signs and miracles He performed for us at that time were contrary to the laws of nature.

The principle of creation "ex nihilo" - out of nothing - is a mighty pillar of our faith and Torah. People who think the world [was not created, but] rather always existed, have no share in the World to Come with Yisrael.

G-d wanted to confer the merit of this noble mitzvah on every Jew, letting no mishap deter him from observing it. Therefore, if one meets with misfortune and cannot bring [the *korban Pesach*] in Nissan, he can bring it in Iyar. Since this is based on a fundamental Torah principle, the obligation even applies to a proselyte who converted between the first and the second *korban Pesach*. One who becomes bar mitzvah between the two Pesach offerings is obligated in this mitzvah as well.

MITZVAH 384 ~ מצוה שפד

TO SOUND TRUMPETS

———◆———

[I]t is a mitzvah] to sound trumpets in the Beis Hamikdash daily, during the offering of every sacrifice, and likewise in time of [national] crisis, as it says, *When you go to war against an enemy who attacks you in your land, you shall sound short blasts on the trumpets* (*Bamidbar* 10:9), and it says in the next verse, *On your days of rejoicing, on your festivals, and on your new-moon celebrations, you shall sound a note with your trumpets for your burnt offerings and your peace offerings.*

It is well-known that an offering becomes unfit through certain disqualifying thoughts. Furthermore, an offering requires complete focus on the Master of the universe, Who commanded us to bring [this offering]. Likewise, in time of trouble, a person must concentrate fully when pleading with his Creator to have mercy on him, rescuing him from his plight. Therefore, we were commanded to sound trumpets at these times. Man of flesh and blood, needs encouragement [to concentrate on matters of the spirit]. Without inspiration, the human nature remains quiescent, and nothing rouses a person like stirring music and the blast of trumpets, which is the loudest of all musical instruments.

Besides inspiring complete focus, the blast of trumpets drives away thoughts of worldly interests, and a person will pay sole attention to the offering.

115

MITZVAH 385 ~ מצוה שפה

TO TAKE CHALLAH

———◦◉◦———

[I]t is a mitzvah] to separate *challah* from each batch of dough, giving it to a kohen, as it says, *From the first portion of your dough you must separate challah as an elevated gift* (*Bamidbar* 15:20).

Since man's life depends on food, and most of the world is sustained with bread, G-d wanted to confer merit on us through a constant mitzvah with our bread. The bread is blessed through this mitzvah and thus the dough becomes food for the body and the soul.

Additionally, the kohanim, who are the servants of Hashem serving Him constantly, will be sustained by [the *challah*] without any effort on their part. This is in contradistinction to the *terumah* which is given to the kohanim as grain which they have to sift and grind.

MITZVAH 386 ~ מצוה שפו

To Wear Tzitzis

<hr>

[T]he Torah commands us] to insert tzitzis in the garments we wear, as it says, *Have them make tzitzis* (*Bamidbar* 15:38). This obligation applies when the garment has four corners or more, as it says, *on the four corners of your garment* (*Devarim* 22:12)

The reason for this mitzvah is explicit in the Torah, *so that we should remember and do all the mitzvos of Hashem.* The greatest aid to memory is carrying one's master's seal attached to the garments he wears constantly, so his eyes and heart are on it all day, as expressed in the verse, *You shall remember all of Hashem's commandments* (*Bamidbar* 15:40).

Our Sages said the [numeric value of] the word *tzitzis* alludes to the 613 mitzvos,[16] if you include the eight threads and the five knots [of the tassel.]

Tzitzis symbolize that man's body and soul are dedicated to Hashem. The white of the threads [of the *tzitzis*] allude to the body, which is made of earth which was created from white snow, as we find in *Pirkei d'Rabbi Eliezer,* "From what was the earth created? From snow that is beneath the Throne of Glory." The threads themselves also hint to the body, because initially, the

---

16 *tzadi*=90 + *yud*=10 + *tzadi*=90 + *yud*=10 + *tav*=400. 90+10+80+10+400 = 600+8+5=613

embryo resembles threads, as Rav Amram in the Gemara *Niddah* said, "Its two thighs are like two threads of red silk, and its two arms are like two threads of red silk."

The *techeiles* [thread is blue,] resembling the sky, to represent the soul that stems from the higher worlds. Our Sages hinted at this, saying, "Why is *techeiles* different from all other colors? Because *techeiles* resembles the sea, the sea resembles the sky, and the sky resembles the Throne of Glory, as it says, *They saw a vision of the G-d of Yisrael, and under His feet was something like a sapphire brick, like the essence of a clear blue sky* (*Shemos* 24:10), and it says also, *The appearance of a sapphire stone in the likeness of a throne* (*Yechezkel 1:26)*." The souls of the righteous are kept underneath the Throne of Glory. For this reason the Sages said that the thread of *techeiles* is wound around the white threads, for the soul comes from the higher [worlds], while the body is of the lower [world].

MITZVAH 387 ~ מצוה שפז

NOT TO STRAY AFTER THE HEART
AND THE EYE

We must not stray after the thoughts of the heart and the sight of the eyes, as it says, *You will then not stray after your heart and after your eyes, which in the past have led you to immorality* (*Bamidbar* 15:39).

This negative commandment deters us from reflecting on theories opposed to the fundamental principles of the Torah, which lead to heresy. If a glimmer of these harmful beliefs enters one's mind, one must banish it, reflecting instead on the true and good ways of the Torah.

Furthermore, one may not chase after [indecent] sights or pursue worldly desires, for they bring evil, disgrace and rage in their wake. The Sages expounded: *You will then not stray after your heart*—refers to heresy; *and after your eyes*—refers to immorality, as it says, *Shimshon said to his father, "Take her for me; for she is fitting in my eyes"* (*Shoftim* 14:3).

Obviously, this protects a person from sinning against Hashem all his life. This mitzvah is a fundamental principle of our faith, since evil thoughts are the father of defilement, with [evil] deeds being their offspring. If the father dies before fathering children, there are no offspring. Consequently, this restriction is the root from which all good things sprout.

My son, our Sages said, "One sin leads to another sin, and one mitzvah leads to another mitzvah." Satisfying your evil desire once, stimulates you [to gratify your craving] many times. But if a strong man suppresses his impulses, he can do it again and again, because desire draws the flesh as wine draws its drinkers. Alcoholics can never drink enough wine; they are always thirsty for more, and the more addicted they become, the stronger is their craving for it. Would they drink only one cup of water, the burning fire of desire for wine would cool, and life would be sweet for them.

Similarly, if a person is addicted to physical pleasure, constantly indulging in it, his evil impulse grows stronger day by day. But if he abstains, he will be happy with his lot, recognizing that G-d made man simple, but they sought many intrigues without any benefit.

MITZVAH 395 ~ מצוה שצה

THE FIRST TITHE

B'nei Yisrael must give one part in ten from the crops of their land to the Levi'im, as it says, *The inheritance that I have given to the Levi'im shall consist of the tithes of B'nei Yisrael which they separate as an elevated gift to Hashem* (*Bamidbar* 27:30), and it says, *The land's tithes . . . are thus consecrated to Hashem* (*Vayikra* 27:30). This is called the First Tithe.

Because Hashem chose the tribe of Levi for His constant service in the Beis Hamikdash, He gave them their sustenance in an honorable way. It is fitting for the servants of the King to have their table set and their meals prepared for them, so they need only toil in the precious service of the King.

Were [the grain] divided into equal portions, the *Levi'im* would be entitled to one twelfth [of the grain], since there were twelve tribes. Nevertheless, their portion is greater than all the others, because as the staff of the King's palace, it is appropriate that their share be greater for their honor. Additionally, the one tenth share comes to them [without deducting] the farmer's expenses.

Whoever sustains the servants of G-d with his resources will find Hashem's blessing reaching all his possessions. The Sages expressed it as follows, "The tithes are a [protective] fence for wealth." They also said, "A person is forbidden to calculate, saying, 'I'll test Hashem, seeing if He grants me good when I involve myself with

His mitzvos. About this [attitude] it says, *Do not test Hashem your G-d* (*Devarim* 6:16). However, this mitzvah [of giving tithes], is an exception; a person was permitted to test if G-d will bless him when he diligently observes it. The prophets said explicitly, *Bring the full tithe into the storehouse . . . and thus put Me to the test, if I will not open for you the windows of heaven, pouring out a blessing upon you* (*Malachi* 3:10)."

MITZVAH 420 ~ מצוה תכ

To Recite the Shema

———◦◉◦———

We are commanded to recite the verse, *Listen, Yisrael, Hashem is our G-d, Hashem is One* (*Devarim* 6:1) every evening and morning. Regarding this verse it says, *Speak of them . . . when you lie down and when you get up* (ibid, 6:7).

Hashem wants to confer merit on His people, having them accept His absolute sovereignty and His oneness, every day and night as long as they live. Man, of flesh and blood, is tempted by the futility of the world and drawn by his cravings. He therefore needs a constant reminder of the kingship of Heaven to guard him from sin.

To make us worthy [of His blessing,] G-d commanded us to remember Him regularly at these two times with total concentration. [We say the Shema] during the day to elevate our daytime activities, remembering the oneness and kingship of Hashem; that His Divine supervision and mastery extends over everything; and that [G-d] sees everything we do, and counts all our steps, with no action or thought hidden from Him. The daytime Shema is one's verbal affirmation of this, protecting him the entire day, while the nighttime Shema serves as protection for the night.

Our sages obligated us to recite the Shema with concentration of the heart; if one did not concentrate, one did not fulfill his obligation.

123

MITZVAH 421 ~ מצוה תכא

THE ARM-TEFILLIN

———◆———

[W]e are commanded] to bind *tefillin* on the arm, as it says, *Bind [these words] as a sign on your hand* (*Devarim* 6:8).

Man, due to his physical nature, tends to pursue whatever is pleasurable and satisfying, like a horse and like a mule without understanding. The soul which G-d granted him, tries to restrain him from sinning. But since [the soul] is locked inside earthly matter, far away from its heavenly realm, it cannot subdue [man's physical nature]; the pull [of the material world] is always greater. And because [the soul] is within the territory [of man's physicality] and subject to its control, it needs protection from [the physical nature,] its evil neighbor.

G-d therefore commanded us to post powerful guards around [our soul]. These [guards] are the commands to study Torah day and night; to attach four *tzitzis* on the four corners of our garments; to affix a *mezuzah* on our doors; and to put *tefillin* on our arms and heads. These guards remind us to withdraw our hands from oppression, so we are not led astray by our eyes and the impulse of our innermost thoughts.

Dear son, our body is much stronger than our soul, for even with all these [safeguards in place, our physical temptations] rise up at times, breaking through these fences. May G-d in His kindness come to our aid, protecting us from them.

MITZVAH 438 ~ מצוה תלח

GRACE AFTER MEALS

———⊷◉⊶———

[I]t is a mitzvah] to bless Hashem after eating one's fill of bread or of the seven species [of produce] mentioned in the Torah. Bread means a loaf of wheat, barley, spelt, oats, or rye. Regarding the seven species it says, *When you eat and are satisfied, you must bless Hashem your G-d, for the good land He has given you* (*Devarim* 8:10).

All honor and glory, good and wisdom, ability and blessing, belong to G-d. Man's speech and actions whether good or bad, do not add to or detract from Him. When we say, "Blessed are you Hashem," or, "He shall be blessed," we do not wish to add blessing to G-d. He does not need anything, for He is Master over everything, and all blessings originate from Him. He provides abundantly wherever His Goodness desires. We must try to understand this concept, or else all the time we spend [on prayers] will be wasted without understanding what we are doing.

Although I am inspiring you [to work on this concept,] I don't believe my intellect is truly capable of understanding even a drop in the ocean of this concept, for I have heard from great scholars that these concepts are based on deep axioms and wondrous secrets that Torah scholars impart to their intelligent and worthy students, whose deeds are pleasant. However, my great desire to acquire some understanding compels me to address this topic.

Hashem created all that exists. He created man, giving him dominion over the earth and everything in it. He has abundant kindness, desiring the well-being of His people, wishing them to be worthy and deserving of His goodness. This stems from His perfection; one perfect in goodness, is one who benefits others.

Thus we may say, that we recite a blessing before Him only to inspire ourselves with our spoken words that He is the blessed One, incorporating all goodness. When we are inspired to acknowledge that He is the source of all goodness, we become worthy of drawing His blessing on us. Accordingly, [when we say, "You are blessed,"] the word "blessed" is a noun, meaning that He incorporates all blessing.

When we say, "He shall be blessed," we are pleading to Him that He cause the hearts of His creations to stand properly before Him acknowledging Him; thereby they will be praised. Thus, "He shall be blessed," means, "May it be Your will that everyone attribute all blessing to You, admitting that everything emanates from You." When everyone acknowledges this, His blessing rests on the world and His desire to do good to others is fulfilled.

The sages said, "The Holy One, blessed is He, desires the prayers of the righteous." This is also to be understood in this vein. He desires that they pray in order that they become worthy to draw down on themselves His goodness, for He wishes to do kindness, conferring blessings out of His great perfection.

———◦◉◦———

[**T**]he Torah commands us] to chase away a mother-bird from its nest before taking the young, as it says, *You must first chase away the mother, and only then may you take the sons* (*Devarim* 22:7).

G-d watches over mankind closely, with individual supervision, as it says, *For His eyes are upon man's ways, and He sees all his steps* (*Iyov* 34:21), whereas He supervises other living creatures in a general way, desiring the survival of every species. Therefore, no species will ever become extinct, for with Divine supervision [all forms of life] will continue to exist.

Reflecting on this, a person will recognize that the continued existence of all forms of life in this world is only by His desire. Not one of [the species] has become extinct and perished, from the eggs of lice to the horns of a *re'eim*-ox, since creation. By the same token, one realizes that by keeping the mitzvos of the Creator, [behaving] with clean hands and a pure heart, G-d will watch over him, keeping him in good health in this world, and keeping his soul alive forever in the World to Come.

About this idea the Sages coined the phrase, "Measure for measure." One who realizes that life and well-being are [determined] only by G-d's supervision, will merit G-d's favor, with good health. The Sages said a person is rewarded for believing in G-d's existence and boundless mastery. By observing the mitzvah [of sending away the mother bird before taking the young,] a person merits having sons, and his existence continues, since sons are the extension of a man's existence and remembrance. The Torah could merely have said, *You must first chase away the mother bird*; by adding the clause, *and then may you take the sons for yourself*, [the Sages] inferred: [As a reward for chasing away the mother bird,] you will gain sons for yourself.

Thus the Sages said: If someone prays, "Have compassion on us, for You are compassionate, since Your mercies extend even to a bird's nest," he is silenced. For [this mitzvah] is not a matter of compassion, rather [acknowledging Hashem's individual supervision through] the fulfillment of the mitzvah makes us worthy. We silence him because he presents this as compassion, whereas it is a fundamental law. Of course, this does not mean the Holy One, blessed be He, does not have compassion, G-d forbid! He is called the Compassionate One, and the Sages said, "Just as G-d is merciful, so you should be merciful." The Sages meant to differentiate between the compassion in Him and in human beings. Human compassion is a trait implanted in man by the Creator. G-d's compassion is His elementary will, for His wisdom dictated compassion since it is a good quality, and all good things are present with Him.

TO MAKE GUARD-RAILS

We must remove obstructions and hazardous objects from our dwellings, as it says, *You must place a guardrail around your roof* (*Devarim* 22:8). We must build an enclosure around roofs, pits, ditches, and the like, so no creature falls and is hurt.

Hashem oversees the actions of people individually, knowing all their deeds. Whatever happens to them, whether good or bad, happens by His decree and command, according to their merit or guilt. Thus the Sages said, "A person does not bruise his finger down on earth unless it is destined to happen to him in Heaven." Nevertheless, a person must guard himself against circumstances that are bound to happen. G-d created His world, based on the laws of nature, decreeing that fire burns and water extinguishes a flame. Nature also dictates that a large stone falling on a man's head will crush his brain, and if a man falls from a high roof he will die.

G-d breathed a soul of life into the bodies of human beings, with intelligence to guard the body against any mishap. He placed the soul and body under the control of the fundamental [laws of nature], bringing the influence of nature to bear on them.

Because the human body is subject to the laws of nature, [man] is commanded to guard himself against accidents; for the strong forces of nature will prevail if he does not guard himself.

However, G-d granted mastery over the forces of nature to a few people whom He wished to honor, because of their great piety and deep devotion to His ways. These are renowned, saintly personalities, such as the holy Forefathers, and many of their descendants such as Daniel, Chananiah, Mishael, and Azariah and others like them. Originally, nature ruled over them, but because of the sublime loftiness of their souls, they eventually became masters over the forces of nature. Thus Avraham, our father, was cast into the fiery furnace, and emerged unharmed; and the four devout men mentioned above, were thrown into the fiery furnace, yet the hair on their heads was not singed, their cloaks were unaltered, and they did not absorb the smell of fire.

Being sinful, most people do not deserve this. Therefore, the Torah commands us to guard our homes and other places so no accidental death should occur due to our negligence; we must not put our lives in jeopardy relying on a miracle. Indeed the Sages said, "If one relies on a miracle, no miracle will be performed for him." Many passages in Tanach convey this idea. Even when the Jews waged a divinely ordained mitzvah-war, in compliance with Hashem's command, they mapped out their strategy, equipped themselves with weapons, and did everything as if they relied completely on the ways of nature. That was the proper approach. All the truthful men agree that this is so.

GLOSSARY

ADAM HARISHON – Adam the first man
AGGADAH – Homiletic discourses
BEIS HAMIKDASH – Holy Temple
BEN – son of
BERACHAH pl. *BERACHOS* – blessing
BEREISHIS –The Book of Genesis
B'NEI YISRAEL – Children of Israel
CHAGIGAH – A sacrifice of rejoicing brought on Yom Tov
CHAMEITZ – Leavened bread
CHEREM – A ban
ERETZ YISRAEL – The Land of Israel
GEHINNOM – Hell
GEMARA – Talmud
HAGGADAH – The text recited at the Passover Seder
HALACHAH pl. *HALACHOS* – Law
HASHEM – God
HAVDALAH – A declaration of separation between a holy day and a
    weekday
KAREIS – Punishment of premature death
KIDDUSH – A declaration sanctifying the beginning of a holy day
KOHEN pl. *KOHANIM* – Priests, descendants of Aaron
KORBAN – Sacrifice
LEVI'IM – from the tribe of Levi
MASHIACH – The Messiah
MATZAH, pl. *MATZOS* – Unleavened bread
METZORA – One stricken with tzaraas leprosy
MEZUZAH – Parchment scrolls containing the Shema that is placed on
    the doorpost.
MIDRASH – A compilation from the sages, usually expounding on
    Scriptures
MINCHAH – A meal offering
MISHKAN – The Tabernacle
MITZVAH pl. *MITZVOS* – Commandment
NASSI – A leader
NAZIR, NAZIRITE pl. *NEZIRIM* – One who makes a vow to abstain
    from wine and from contact with the dead
NOSAR – The leftovers of a sacrifice after the time to eat it has expired

OMER – An offering of barley brought on the second day of Pesach
ONKELOS – A convert who wrote an Aramaic translation of the Torah
PARASHAS – The portion [of the Torah]
PESACH – Passover
REBBI – Teacher
SANHEDRIN – Jewish High Court
SEFER – Book or scroll
SHAATNEIZ – The prohibition against wearing wool and linen
   combined
SHABBOS – The day of rest, Saturday
SHAVUOS – Festival of Weeks
SHECHINAH – Divine Presence
SHECHITAH – Ritual slaughter
SHEMA – The portion of the Torah containing the declaration of
   Hashem's unity that we are required to recite every morning and
   evening
SHEMITTAH – The sabbatical year when work in the field is prohibited
SHOFAR – Ram's horn blown on Rosh Hashana
SUKKAH – Hut used on Sukkos
SUKKOS – Festival of Tabernacles
TAMEI –Ritually impure
TANACH – Scriptures
TECHEILES – Wool dyed blue
TEFILLIN – Phylacteries
TEHILLIM – Psalms
TEREIFAH – An animal that has been wounded in a way that it will die
   within 12 months
TERUAH – The broken staccato sound of the Shofar
TERUMAH pl. *TERUMOS* – Contribution to the Kohein
TESHUVAH – Repentance
TUM'AH – Ritual impurity
TZADDIK pl. *TZADDIKIM* – Pious Person
TZARAAS – Leprosy
TZEDAKAH – Charity
TZITZIS – Fringes worn on a four cornered garment
VAYIKRA – The Book of Leviticus
YAMIM TOVIM – Holidays
YERUSHALAYIM – Jerusalem
YISRAEL – Israel
YITZCHOCK – Isaac
YOM TOV – Holiday
YOVEL – The jubilee year